Cathy Hayes was born in Isl after obtaining her GCSEs. Ir tration clerk, she progressed a contract as a clinical manager

She decided to start her own eBay business and kept a diary to record her efforts. Struck by her early success, the author inspired many of her friends and family to set up eBay businesses of their own and hopes that the publication of this book will inspire many more.

Other titles from How To Books

THE SMALL BUSINESS START-UP WORKBOOK
Cheryl D. Rickman

START AND RUN A GREETING CARDS BUSINESS
Elizabeth White

START AND RUN A SUCCESSFUL BEAUTY SALON
Sally Medcalf and Bijan Yousef Zadeh

WRITE YOUR OWN BUSINESS PLAN
Paul Hetherington

A ONE PERSON BUSINESS
Clive Morton

The Easy eBay Business Guide

Cathy Hayes

RIGHT WAY

Constable & Robinson Ltd
55–56 Russell Square
London WC1B 4HP
www.constablerobinson.com

First published in the UK by Right Way,
an imprint of Constable & Robinson Ltd., 2014

NOTE: The material contained in this book is set out in good faith for general
guidance and no liability can be accepted for loss or expense incurred as a result of
relying in particular circumstances on statements made in the book. Laws and
regulations are complex and liable to change, and readers should check the current
position with relevant authorities before making personal arrangements

A copy of the British Library Cataloguing in
Publication data is available from the British Library

ISBN 978-1-84528-524-1 (paperback)
ISBN 978-1-84528-529-6 (ebook)

Printed and bound in the UK

1 3 5 7 9 10 8 6 4 2

CONTENTS

CONTENTS

CONTENTS

ACKNOWLEDGEMENTS

There are many people who influenced the writing of this book and I hope that I have managed to list them all.

To our children, Lauren, Jamie, Kane and Ned – my world, my happiness, my favourite wrappers – and to my mum, Caroline McCarty, for all the support.

For everyone involved in my company's growth: Azad Ahmad, Ramz, Alex Miah, Beata Orzechowska, Luke Grayston, Marlon the Postie, Newel, Dinesh, Ishmal, Leon Perkin, Sue Levy, Breannan Baker, Michel, Ray Featherstone, Claire Alexander, Phaedra Horton, Georgia Hepper and Justin Morris.

My cousin Jen McCarty and my friend Prab Atwal for inspiring me to write this book.

My friends in beautiful Jamaica – until we meet again …

Most of all I want to thank my partner, my everything – John Comber … thank you for believing in me and putting up with me while we created this guide.

FOREWORD

I have witnessed at first hand the dedication and tenacity displayed by your author, who is an inspirational woman. Cathy, my partner in both business and life, has always strived to improve herself. She is both ambitious and hardworking, and as such puts in the effort to achieve her goals.

Inspired by her success, I have since opened a shop of my own which is growing nicely. I have employed the same systems and methods as Cathy and they work perfectly for me. Cathy has also advised several friends who were looking for employment or a bit of extra spare cash, and they have all entered into the world of eBay.

Cathy intends to launch a mentoring programme to teach the skills she has acquired while building and running her business. She has seen that in today's economic climate many people are struggling to make ends meet or losing their jobs and has decided to offer this service and launch her book to give them an opportunity to generate an income for themselves.

In the book, Cathy tells her own story about the launch, build and success of her first year in business and then shows you how to do it for yourself in a very easy to follow, step-by-step guide.

Cathy's story should inspire anyone to take the bull by the horns and start up a business. It is possible to achieve a good income in a relatively short space of time if her rules are adhered to. There are hundreds of pointers and snippets of advice that will speed up your processes and make your listings look great. In my opinion, this book is a must buy for anyone who wants to start a 'Buy it Now' business on ebay.co.uk.

John Comber

PREFACE

By following the guide, you should be able to achieve an income in a very short space of time by avoiding the mistakes I made and practising the procedures I have adopted. There are huge savings to be made in both time and money by using my step-by-step guide to set up accounts in the right places and employ the systems that I have devised.

The guide is an easy and straightforward process telling you exactly what you need to know. I have tried to keep it as short and to the point as possible so as not to overwhelm you with information that isn't relevant to the operation.

Some people learn best through real and concrete experiences while others learn by seeking advice, discussing a matter with others, receiving instructions or watching someone else perform the task. Still others learn through abstract, conceptualisation involving the study of others, models, systems or simulations of the real world. Finally, some people learn through actual experimentation. They like to try new behaviours and the result is that they learn by doing.

Despite the differences in how people learn, we know that the maximum benefit received from training doesn't always come from learning something new. Rather, it comes from learning to do better what one already does well. The real goal then is to encourage people to do better what they are already good at and to allow them to teach others their successful habits and work patterns.

If I can help just a few people out of trouble and enable them to gain some control back in their lives, then my work is done. I once read somewhere that it is far more rewarding to give than to receive and this, I think, is the motivation behind writing this book.

PART I

A Year in the Life of an eBay Virgin

1
HOW IT ALL BEGAN

Like everybody out there I had rummaged through my old stuff, what I thought was rubbish, cleaned it up and sold it on eBay. I'd even gone as far as to actually pick things up in markets that I thought had the potential to make more and often did, and so maybe that was when the seed was sown. It wasn't, however, until a long time later that I decided to become a fully fledged eBay seller and so this story began.

I had been working, very happily, for the National Health Service as an administration and clerical manager and was absolutely devastated when my contract came to an end. I worked in other departments casually for the next few months but just couldn't manage to secure a full-time and permanent position no matter how hard I tried and in the end I just got fed up, to be frank, with my desperation for it.

In January 2010, my friend Sarah and I had met for lunch at the hospital where I worked and after our trip to the canteen we went to take a look at a book stall that was erected in the foyer, outside the hospital canteen. As we browsed around Sarah picked up a copy of a CD by a lady called Doreen Virtue, which was titled *Manifesting with Angels*.

A few weeks after Sarah purchased the CD I was at her house while she was looking for a new property as she had to leave the one she had been renting. As I nosed through a bundle of property particulars on her kitchen table, I stumbled across one that looked perfectly suitable and, after a call to the agent, we discovered the house was available to view. Sarah eventually secured the tenancy and moved in, but what was really strange was that while she had been listening to that Doreen Virtue CD, she had visualised moving on to the street where that very house was situated.

Fascinated by what Sarah had told me, at the very beginning of March 2010 I returned home from work and went on to eBay and decided to purchase the Doreen Virtue CD for myself. It arrived within a few days and, as you will see below in my feedback history, the story unfolds.

The CD arrived and when I began listening to it, I was asked to visualise where I would be a year from now and what I would be doing. I began imagining that I would be helping others in some way to learn a new skill that would help them out of a rut. The result is this book, which I hope will help you succeed as an eBay seller in the same way that I have.

As you can see from the following table, the seller of the Angels CD left me feedback on 7 March 2010 and I received the CD the next day. Just a short time later I received my very first feedback as a professional seller on eBay for the Dualit DAB Radio, which is when my professional eBay feedback score began.

✚	Great product super fast delivery. Fastest Ever!! Best eBay seller ever!! :-)	Buyer: ★★★★★★★ 89	10–Apr–10 09:53
	Dualit DAB Lite Kitchen Radio FM/DAB DLR1 90200 Chrome (#140392722228)	£87.99	
✚	★★THANK YOU ★★ MEDIA- BARROW VALUES YOUR CUSTOM★★	Seller: ★★★★★★_★★★★★★ 42788	07–Mar–10 14:50
	MANIFESTING WITH THE ANGELS CD AUDIO (#360238117162)	--	

On 28 February 2010, just a week before first listening to Doreen Virtue's CD, I was having lunch at my desk in the Executive Offices at the hospital and I read an article about some very successful eBay traders overseas and that was it. On arriving home that evening I nagged John (my personal and business partner) into submission to help me rummage through the loft and understair cupboard collecting everything I could list. From a Worcester Boiler to a buggy, and an old telephone to a coffee machine, the listings began. After a seven-day auction of our old stuff, we had sold it all and came away with a very handsome £600 profit. I was hooked!

In the coming weeks, during my lunch hours at work I would scour through eBay looking at what sold well and I then recorded the data on to a research chart that I devised with items that sold well, how many, how much for, etc.

With this information in tow I moved on to car-boot sales and markets, buying anything I thought would sell.

Product (S Kitchen App)	Condn	Source & Price	eBay Price	Bids
Cuisinart Ice Cream Maker (up to 1L)	Used		£67.50 £15.00 pp	16
Cuisinart Ice Cream Maker (up to 1L)	Used		£197.99 Free pp	18
Kenwood Smoothie Maker	Used As New		£12.50 Pick up	6
Philips Juicer Aluminium Colln			£41.00 £20.00 pp	7
Electric Waffle Maker – Silvercrest	New		£12.33 £6.99 pp	29
EasiYo Real Yogurt/ Maker Starter Pack	New		£15.92 Free pp	14
Potato Peeler Att. Kenwood Chef A801			£26.00 £4.99 pp	15
Kenwood Chef A901 Food Mixer	Used		£86.00 £13.00 pp	19
Bamix Food Mixer Hand-held			£34.03 £5.00 pp	11
Hinari Chrome/Pink Toaster High Lift	Used		£21.00 £4.99 pp	9
Gaggia Classic Coffee Maker	Used		£114.06 £15.00 pp	10
Kenwood Café Retro Coffee Maker			£36.00 Free pp	10
Nespresso Magimix M200 Coffee Maker			£54.98 £10.00 pp	11
Rancilio Silvia Espresso Machine	New		£287.00 £15.00 pp	30
Tassimo Coffee Maker TAS40xx	New		£77.55 £10.00 pp	8
Pavoni Europiccola Espresso Machine	Used		£207.50 £12.00 pp	19
Ascaso I-Mini Coffee Grinder	New		£121.00 £15,00 pp	16

HOW IT ALL BEGAN

Product (S Kitchen App)	Condn	Source & Price	eBay Price	Bids
Morphy Richards Accents Kettle	Used		£25.00 £7.00 pp	21
Swan Kettle & 4 Sl Toaster in Red	New		£51.00 £9.00	18
Tefal Quick Cup Kettle	New		£19.00 £5.95 pp	12
Spong Mincer	Used		£11.00 £3.50 pp	9
Cream DeLonghi CT04E 4 sl Toaster	Used		£28.80 £10.00 pp	19
Tefal Jamie Oliver Pressure Cooker	New		£70.00 £6.00 pp	17
Tefal Steamer	Used	£3.00 Car Boot		
Swan Food Steamer	New		£11.05 £3.00 pp	14
Goblin Teasmade	Used	£6.00 Car Boot		
Breville Bread Maker	Used	£5.00 Car Boot		
Philips Teasmade	Used	£3.00 Car Boot		
Kenwood Smoothie Hot/Cold	Used	£7.00 Car Boot		
Kenwood Smoothie Maker	Used	£7.00 Car boot		
Alessi Aldo Rossi Kettle	Used		£54.00 £15.00 pp	9

Product (Children Safety)	Condn	Source & Price	eBay Price	Bids
Polyotter Inflatable Float Suit Age 2-4	New in Box		£4.00 £2.50 pp	8
Splash About Float Jacket Age 1-3	Used		£15.10 £2.50 pp	21

Product (Baby/Maternity)	Condn	Source & Price	eBay Price	Bids
Dream Genii Pregnancy Pillow	New		£35.00 £5.29 pp	17
La Bassine Birthing Pool Made in Water	New		£78.00 £20.00 pp	21
Avent Baby Bottles Starter Kit	New		£16.00 £4.00 pp	7
Wireless Digital Baby Monitor 2.5 LCD	New		£79.99 £9.99 pp	1
Angelcare Movement & Sound Monitor	New		£51.00 £6.50 pp	10
Blue LCD Display Fetal Doppler	New		£17.00 £3.99 pp	28

Product (Misc)	Condn	Source & Price	eBay Price	Bids
Pair of 6 in G Clamps By Woden			£10.50 £10.00 pp	4
Black Kickers Size 5	New		£37.01 £3.50	15
Black Kickers Size 6	New		£41.00 £5.90 pp	13
Kickers	Used	£3.00 Car Boot		
Converse Shoes (Beige)	Used	£5.00 Charity Shop		
Converse Boots (Pink)	As New	£10.00 Car Boot		
Converse Boots (Black)	Used	Mine from home		
Running Shoes Size 4	Used			
Dunlop Shoes Size 4	Used	Mine from home		

Books on Abuse	Used	£2.00 Charity Shop		
Car Chargers x 3	New	£3.00 £Shop		
Mountain Buggy Breeze	Used	Mine from home		
Double Panasonic Phone Set	Used	Mine from home		

Product (Outdoor Pursuits)	Condn	Source & Price	eBay Price	Bids
Campingaz Stove 206s/1200w	New Boxed		£4.40 £1.50 pp	13
Igloo Cool Box MaxCold 5	Used		£60.00 Pick up	19
Halfords Electric Cool Box 18 litre	Used but as new		£19.00 Free	19
Lowa Men's Tarnark Backpacking Boots	New No Box		£105.34 £60.20 pp	20
LED Lenser P7 Torch	Used		£33.00 £1.85 pp	8
Suunto Core Black Watch SS014279010	New		£153.97 Free pp	23
Surefire E2DL 200 Lumers Flashlight	New		£92.72 Free pp	14
Snow Peak Titanium Bowls	Used		£20.50 £2.50 pp	12
Skandika Milano 6b Family Tent	New		£303.00 £19.00 pp	33

Product (S Kitchen Acc)	Condn	Source & Price	eBay Price	Bids
Kenwood Chef Pyrex Mixing Bowl	Used		£14.70 £4.95 pp	9
4 Square Cake Tins Wedding (1971–2)	Used		£27.00 £10.00 pp	10
Tefal Actua 6 pce Non-Stick Pan Set	New		£47.67 £9.00 pp	12
Water Softener Permutt PSM65 V2	New		£262.00 £15.00 pp	15
Brita Classic Water Filter Cartridges	New		£16.50 £6.00 pp	13
Avery Kitchen Scales & Brass Weights	Used		£18.22 £11.00 pp	7
Worcester Greenstar 12RI Boiler	Used		£220.55 Pick up	10
Belfast Butler Sink with Waste Kit	New		£153.00 Pick up	18
WW PR Teapot sugar cream 2 mugs	Used		£530.00 £7.50 pp	15

I also began emailing manufacturers of popular products, trying to find out how I could get hold of their goods straight from the source. This exercise proved tricky and items direct from the manufacturer didn't seem to be coming in much cheaper than on eBay so the markets proved an invaluable source where I could pick up used, good-quality items that I knew would sell (based on my research during work breaks). I would buy the goods, take them home, clean them up and, sometimes with a little help from John, fix them up. Then I would sell them on. This gave me an income to build upon while I continued my research. It also kept me on eBay as a consistent, active and regular professional seller and my all-important feedback grew.

To begin with I had loads of time, even managing to hold down my casual work at the hospital. Every spare day I had involved visits to charity shops, markets, fetes, fairs, in fact anywhere I could get hold of products, and every single product I bought I sold at a profit.

My best buy was a Dualit Filter Coffee Machine that I picked up from a lovely young couple in Holloway car-boot sale for £2. It sold for £52, a 2,500 per cent profit! I could hardly believe my luck.

There was the odd thing that would not work when you got it home from a car-boot sale, but more often than not the people I bought from were honest and happy to refund me if an item was faulty. I became a more and more familiar face at car-boot sales across north London. I knew the stalls that had the good stuff and often they would hold it back for me, giving me a call as and when reliable stock arrived. I even went as far as providing market traders with lists of the items I would buy immediately from them.

My front room and dining room started to resemble something out of *Only Fools and Horses* with different pieces of electrical equipment, waiting to be cleaned and/or repaired, sprawled over every available surface. The kids were increasingly curious, playing with buttons and switches, but eventually they got used to seeing random teasmades or coffee machines lying around and it all became perfectly normal. To them the things I was buying became just part of the furniture and not new toys for them to investigate and take apart!

As time went on, and as profitable as the car-boot sale products were, it was becoming more and more time-consuming to go out, buy a product, take it home, clean it up and possibly repair it on top of then waiting for a seven-day auction to end. At the beginning, I used to watch excitedly as the auction would end to see how much money I had made from my second-hand gems. But soon I was sending out so many products and had so many pending that watching the final seconds of an auction very quickly became a thing of the past.

Sourcing my stock was what took up most of my time and required weeks if not months of exhausting research. The hours were gruelling and the exercise frustrating as I trawled through the internet night after night, and there were many times I really felt like giving up. However, I kept thinking of the bigger picture, remembering how much time and money it would ultimately save me if I could just find some suppliers who would deliver direct to my door, and with every breakthrough my motivation grew. With each new supplier that I added to my growing portfolio, I found that my time researching was now just a part of my daily work routine, and it no longer interfered with my evenings and weekends.

Sometimes I got lucky and was able to find out the contact details of the suppliers to main high-street outlets from the packaging in which they supplied the products (a valuable tip I had also learned from the internet) so my eyes were wide open at all times. Some of my biggest suppliers were sourced using this exact method.

Once I had built relationships with my suppliers, I began to negotiate prices with them. I realised that they were as keen to sell to me as I was to buy from them. I learnt very quickly that the saying 'if you don't ask you don't get' is absolutely true. My suppliers often had large quantities of a product that was an end of line or season stock that they were desperate to clear in order to make space for their more current lines. I made a point of going to meet suppliers personally, no matter how far away they were, and this exercise proved very worthwhile.

If your supplier knows you personally, you will be amazed at the deals they will offer, and especially if you place an order direct from their showroom. Being in the showroom also gave me a better understanding of products I wanted to purchase. I sat one day for hours with my laptop in a supplier's showroom with tens of potential new products, researching them and ordering them while being served coffee and biscuits all day long.

I was like a kid in a sweet shop that day and added thirty new lines to my shop. By visiting the supplier's showroom, I gained a completely new perspective on the products I had previously viewed online. I suppose it's a bit like looking for a house on the internet and then viewing it in real life. Your perspective and expectation is always very different and it was the same principle with my stock. Some items looked much better in reality and some much worse, and I would often see new lines that weren't even in the supplier's catalogue or website because they were brand new or end of the line goods.

On Mother's Day 2010, John, myself and the kids went out with my brother Matt and his family for a pub lunch in Highgate and while talking about my very new eBay shop, my brother happened to mention an Argos clearance website that sold off pallets of old stock. Naturally, I was curious about this so after feeding, bathing and putting the children to bed that night, I started to surf the internet looking for the site.

I found the website, but the pallets were far too big and expensive for a very inexperienced and relatively poor business like mine so I dismissed the opportunity. However, because I had put the words 'auction' and 'clearance' in the search engine, other potential suppliers came up that I hadn't seen before, and one in particular caught my eye. It was an 'auction room' style website where you could bid on graded bankrupt and returned stock and it was a lot like eBay in that you had to bid for a pallet.

One day while visiting my mum I nervously watched as the timer ticked down to the end and in the last ten seconds I hit the 'Buy Now' key. In the click of a button I had just purchased my very first pallet of D-grade Dualit stock. A call came literally minutes later from the company to confirm that I was the winning bidder and the pallet arrived on my driveway the next morning. My first and most immediate thought was … where on earth am I going to put all these kettles? It was a bit of a risk buying a D-grade pallet but I needn't have worried: 90 per cent of the goods were new and in perfect condition with damage being confined just to the packaging.

Of the remaining 10 per cent, some were used but working, and after a bit of a clean were suitable for sale. We mixed and matched the others to repair broken handles or lids and discarded a few that were beyond repair.

At the beginning of April 2010 I received my first eBay feedback as a registered business seller. It came from a very happy lady who had bought one of my Dualit radios (they were so gorgeous I even nicked one for myself): 'Great product super fast delivery. Fastest Ever!! Best eBay seller ever!! :-)'

We had actually cheated a bit with this one. The customer lived almost opposite my baby's nursery in Islington, so my partner John hand-delivered it to her door on the morning after she had purchased it from us just the previous night.

It was a great omen and that first feedback led to more than 12,000 positive feedbacks in just shy of a year.

The return on the Dualit stock was good and in less than a month it was gone and my understair cupboard was ready for another delivery.

In the meantime, however, in the first week of April and just days after the first pallet was delivered, again, quite by chance, the whole direction of my new company changed. My partner John and I were at a discount store buying some treats for our little boys when we stumbled across a camping mat. John suggested we might be able to sell it on eBay and into the basket it went. We then went on to buy many more once our research checks on eBay confirmed that we could in fact sell this product and more than double our money. We wiped the shelves in both our local store and neighbouring stores, with, I can assure you, very puzzled looks from both the staff and fellow customers. We made our first camping-mat sale on 6 April 2010 and it remains one of our biggest sellers to this day along with mosquito repellent that we also purchased from the same shop!

At the till I would always get endless questions from other customers. Some would come right out and just ask why we were buying so many mats, whereas others would ask in a less intrusive way, i.e. 'Are you going on a camping trip?' I was always such a terrible liar, especially when put on the spot like that, so I simply told them the truth, which led to so many questions, while the parking meter ticked away outside!

At the very beginning, one lady asked me for the name of my eBay shop and I just spontaneously replied 'C&J Trading'. As I drove home I wondered if it was the most sensible idea to give out the name of my shop when she was taking such a close interest in the stock in my basket. In the midst of my paranoia and panic, and after John confirmed that it was a less than clever idea to give away such information, we very hastily changed the name of our shop to one that I loathed ... 'Value for Money Emporium'.

It was such a mouthful and I cringed every time I uttered it to anybody. Suffice to say, that shop title didn't stick around for very long either.

I was now feeling a little more confident as a professional seller, having sold off one pallet with several other lines listed from our discount store finds. So on 12 April 2010 I took delivery of a second pallet from another wholesaler I had found, this time full of camping equipment, perfect for the summer season ahead. The stock, again, was all customer returns, and again we got lucky with the standard of the goods that arrived.

I remember arriving home from work to a dining room full of stock, not knowing quite what we were letting ourselves in for, but I felt compelled to keep going, realising that we were on to something good. It seemed I just knew what I had to do and the only thing holding me back was space, which remains an issue to this very day.

As my sales increased with items I had bought from our local discount store, I inevitably became a regular face and within weeks was on first name terms with Alex, the store manager. He was a little bemused with my activity and curious to know what exactly I was doing with all his stock. I would often rush around the store frantically, all the time worrying that my parking meter would expire as with each trip I'd spend longer and longer unearthing new lines that I could add to my ever expanding shop.

After a few weeks, as our relationship developed, Alex offered me the opportunity to park at the rear of the store and that took everything up a gear, saving me a huge amount of anxiety and time.

I no longer needed to rush or worry about parking-tickets, so I now wandered around the store with my camera (with Alex's permission), sometimes for hours, taking photos of potential stock opportunities. Using my camera research, I was able to decipher possible lines very quickly and effectively, making manual lists on bits of paper for items to purchase and deleting those from my phone that were not suitable for resale. This saved me the enormous amount of time I had spent buying and returning potential lines, and Alex was happy, too, as I was no longer turning up, receipt in hand, with huge bagfuls of returns.

Using the camera was fine at his store, but unfortunately not all store managers were so happy with this arrangement. On one occasion a security guard asked me to put my camera away or else he would confiscate it or ask me to leave the shop!

As I added more and more lines, I was finding it increasingly difficult to hold down my casual work at the hospital. I would try to list items during my lunch break and during quiet periods, but it just wasn't working, so I eventually had to give up my job and was now able to concentrate on eBay full time. That day was the catalyst for the speed at which the company grew after that, trying to master the competitive world of eBay trading.

By this stage I was adding at least five new lines per day and noticed a pattern on my Selling Manager Pro Summary. It seemed that for every new line I added, my twenty-four hour sales figure would rise by £1, so if I had 100 lines running my figure would read £100 per day and so on.

As you can imagine, this made the urge to add more lines even more irresistible and I slowly became addicted to finding more new products to add to my ever expanding shop.

It was such a buzz to list an item that morning and see it begin selling within hours if not minutes of going live, and with each successful product I listed I just got more drawn in.

It was like I had the key to a big secret and my heart would palpitate with excitement. I felt untouchable, like no one could do it like I could, and with that mindset, the stock just kept on coming and my shelves just kept on emptying.

I started thinking of ways to enhance my products even more, so instead of just selling them individually, I would team-up products to lure the buyer into my shop of bargain buys. Instead of selling just Christmas trees, I decorated them with lights and perhaps an angel on top to sell as a complete package, while still using the decorated picture to offer the tree undecorated too. I looked for inspiration, whether in magazines, catalogues, people's homes, shop windows – in fact, just about anywhere. I even went as far as to decorate my dining table with an entire Christmas setting including tablecloth, napkins, glasses, placemats and crackers, and offered it for sale either as a complete set or as individual items. These combinations became some of my best-sellers during that first Christmas season.

The whole family and some of my friends became my own personal models. John puckered his lips in an irresistible pose for me while wearing a Santa-style hat with a sprig of mistletoe dangling down … it was very fetching. My boys did their bit too, modelling various Santa hats as well as a Christmas apron and chef's hat set with wooden spoons in hand for maximum effect. Although they were very reluctant to start with, the whole experience ended up being thoroughly enjoyable and is something the kids talk about to this day. They love seeing their faces on eBay every Christmas and Halloween, and enjoy telling their friends all about being 'models' for Mummy and to 'go find them on eBay'.

Some of the time, getting the stock ready for photography was incredibly tedious, displaying the trees in all their colours, dressing my dining table or dressing the boys, but my buyers seemed to love our attention to detail and the sales reflected that time and time again.

We had four designs of dried flowers that came in their own individual cardboard display boxes. We photographed all four designs together in a glass vase for extra effect. From that one listing we had literally hundreds of queries from customers enquiring whether they could buy the whole display including the vase!

It was all about standing out from the crowd. I noticed how so many eBay traders would just take an average photograph, sometimes not even removing it from the packaging, and that was not something I wanted to reflect.

I had carefully handpicked my products and spent a lot of my time researching them, so it was very important for me to take pride in each and every item, as I somehow knew this would make them sell even more. What seemed obvious to me just didn't seem obvious at all to most of my competition and the sales reflected that. Month on month my sales increased from 1,000 per month in April 2011 to 2,693 just a year later in April 2012. I had a repeat customer base of 5.5 per cent in June 2010, peaking at 9.4 per cent just five months later in November 2010.

Like products in shop windows of major department stores, I wanted the goods that I was selling to be presented in the best way I could manage. Every product that was packaged was removed from the packaging and, if it was a kitchen product, we would photograph it in our kitchen with my apple green tiles as the backdrop. If it was a general home product we would use our solid oak floor as a background. It was the same for clothing: Santa hats would be modelled by myself or other willing participants, and so on. Umbrellas were photographed both open and closed and they sold like hot cakes.

I don't think I had a single product that didn't sell. There were even times when I noticed other traders selling identical products to me at a lower price, yet mine outsold theirs tenfold because of my title, my presentation and my ever-expanding reputation as a fast and powerful Top Rated Seller on eBay.

With other title listings, for example, we would find some sellers leaving out vital information from size right through to colour. They would waste vital characters with nonsense descriptive terms, leaving out the specifics, which meant they sold nothing at all. At the beginning (and even now when doing my personal shopping on eBay), I often find myself purchasing really badly listed items. I am normally the only bidder because of the quality of the listing and I go on to sell it for, sometimes, twenty times the price I have paid for it originally. I believe one of the UK's biggest eBay sellers actually started trading in exactly that way, buying badly listed PlayStation consoles.

I figured that there had to be a reason why high-street stores spend millions on marketing for their in-store catalogues or shop windows, and if it worked for them it could work for me too. Even when I was buying from the discount stores, my mind kept telling itself that if they can sell these products at such low prices, yet still pay rent, rates, staff, VAT and all the other overheads associated with running a shop, and still walk away with a profit, then surely eBay could generate a little profit too. Yes, I would have the PayPal fees, eBay fees and postage and packing (P&P) costs, but the P&P costs were going back to the buyers and, anyhow, the overheads didn't compare to high-street rent, rates, staff and so on.

It seemed to me that the pure generation of profit lay in the sheer volume these stores were pushing out nationally throughout their company. I knew that eBay was open to a whole different and independent community of its own that I could tap into, and the icing on the cake was that it was international too.

I was often surprised when some of my buyers lived, quite literally, opposite some of the shops I was purchasing my products from, yet paying a premium for them from me on eBay rather than venturing inside the store. Perhaps they were just oblivious to the fact they could buy the same product at a nearby shop or maybe they simply weren't the type of people to use such stores! Nevertheless, I of course welcomed their custom and their positive feedback, which just kept on coming. However, my main target market wasn't going to be the city buyer, but more the out-of-towners who lived in the remotest parts of the country.

I was so used to living in a city where anything was accessible to me within a three-mile radius, and taking that 'city girl' status for granted, I'd never before really considered the difficulties for people living in other parts of Britain. It was while walking around IKEA that it suddenly occurred to me that many people not only didn't have access to bargain discount stores but more than likely didn't have access to the bigger out-of-town stores like IKEA, Lidl, Aldi and Primark either, especially if they didn't have a car. These stores, unlike Argos for example, were not on every town high street, but were dotted around retail parks in selective areas. This meant there was room to expand for me and my company.

As time went on, I began to realise that just by looking at my despatch notes how a high percentage of my customers were coming from the areas I was targeting.

I researched the out-of-town retail park stores more and more, and after a while I learnt that some didn't even deliver unless you had a minimum spend, which alienated the small-purchase customer even further, so I decided to test my theory out.

I went back to IKEA a few days later and I saw some frying pans that were being sold for £1.49. I bought five, took them home, removed all of the IKEA packaging, listed them as a non-branded, non-stick frying pan at £4.99 + P&P and within just a couple of days I had sold out.

Day by day, we seemed to be spending more time at the post office and during one of our many trips, on 27 April 2010, a fellow customer saw John passing over a large amount of heavy items and piped up from the back of the queue, 'It's much cheaper to send those with Parcel2Go.' It is amazing how people come to your aid at just the right moment. I am a true believer in putting help out there and getting it back.

As soon as we arrived home we searched for the company online and our relationship with courier agents began. This was the first of many systems that worked towards easing our job, protecting our goods and saving us money.

A product that weighed more than 2 kg was now sent by courier and the item was not only collected from our door, but also insured and tracked, and a proof of delivery was obtained, unlike the Royal Mail Standard Parcels service where the item was not tracked or signed for at all. The courier service was substantially cheaper than using Parcelforce with Royal Mail even through the Packetpost system. It would pick up from me on the same day or the next day, depending on the time that I made the booking, and was a reliable and secure way of transporting large or heavy goods.

Our visits to the post office to post smaller items were still increasing, and we were very quickly on first name terms with the postmaster and mistress in Colney Hatch Lane, Muswell Hill, and the busier we got the more accommodating they became. At the beginning we would take one or two IKEA bags full of packages, but week on week the bags grew in numbers until we were taking up to fifteen bags full of packages and parcels to be weighed and stamped.

Right at the very beginning of our venture, John and I were complete novices when it came to eBay trading and wrapped our products in anything that was available, and this was more often than not black bags and A4 brown Manila envelopes. They worked well to begin with, but as the product range expanded we noticing some feedback downgrading from our buyers for 'poor packaging' with the final push coming when our postmistress told us that our packages were regularly splitting.

So on 18 May 2010 we succumbed to the bad ratings and nagging from our postmistress and went, of all places, on to eBay to purchase our very first order of bubble wrap, Sellotape, brown tape, fragile tape and the all-important mailing bags. To this day, I am still unsure why we put it off for so long. Perhaps we were in denial as to the serious nature of our business or just worried about committing to buying large quantities of packaging, but all our worries proved unfounded and we continue to work exclusively with a company called Globe Packaging to this day. Having used several packing suppliers, we found Globe to be the most clear and reliable in despatch time and in the organisation of our order, which was crucial.

After several months of using the company, we phoned the manager to explain the quantities we were buying and suggested sourcing all our packaging materials from him, asking what his best price would be. The final price we negotiated offered us a substantial saving and exclusivity from him, and was a win-win situation for both parties. In summary: consolidate all your supplies with one supplier and save pounds.

His winning formula of attention to detail and competitive pricing secured him an exclusive deal with us and is another fine example of eBay trading being practised correctly and skilfully. Other suppliers, in the past, had sent us mailing bags in different sizes all mixed together inside one box and this led to confusion, which resulted in hours of sorting at our end. With Globe Packaging, the bags were sorted by size category, and the sizing was clearly displayed box by box.

Our packing supplier initially may have been a little more expensive than some others, but for the time he saved us, we were more than happy to pay that little bit extra and, ultimately, we got the best supplier and a better price than any of the other sellers could offer through eBay.

This valuable lesson showed us that the way you pack your item is as important as the way you sell it. It requires consideration for the person who is receiving the goods at the other end. We want the buyer to come to us and NOT the next person selling exactly the same product on eBay, and as our monthly customer figures reveal, they return in abundance. Packaging is an important part of this approach.

The cheaper sellers lost me as a customer that day and who knows how many more they have lost due to lack of attention to detail, and it is plain to see just by looking at the feedback score of the different sellers why this is so crucial to becoming a successful eBay trader.

Customers expect an item to arrive as it would if you were purchasing it from a shop: displayed well, packaged nicely and with product information shown in a clear and concise manner. I knew, from my own personal shopping experiences on eBay, that often people were buying a product as a gift for someone and I had in the past asked the seller to send the item direct to the gift receiver. Therefore, when packaging an item, I would always assume that any of the products I sent could be a potential gift going direct to the gift receiver. I therefore trained myself and my wrappers to wrap a package as if it were a gift going to somebody they loved.

We would always protect each item by wrapping it carefully and thoroughly, whether with tissue paper for items of clothing or bubble wrap and cardboard for more fragile products. For example, if the product was ladies' underwear, I might use a pastel-coloured bag such as pink (widely available). However, if the product was not necessarily for gift purposes (e.g. a car part), then a standard grey bag would suffice.

I managed to contain our lines of products to four different sizes of bags (predominantly grey), which I labelled Small, Medium, Large and Extra Large.

I would always try to limit the amount of cardboard boxes we purchased and generally tried to recycle the ones in which we received our products. We only ever used boxes in exceptional circumstances for items that would not be protected by bubble wrap and tape alone. This was because a box, unless recycled, is far more costly than a bag and piece of bubble wrap.

Sometimes I got lucky with some of my products arriving direct from the supplier individually wrapped inside boxes of their own, ready for despatch. Other than that, common sense and/or trial and error prevailed and after time I was able to decipher which product needed which packaging for all future orders.

At first it was overwhelming, but I was amazed how quickly my brain filed all the information. You will soon know and understand your products, and personally I found making mistakes was the best possible way to learn.

My buyers generally understood if a mistake happened once, or even twice, and if the mistake only happened a couple of times a month it was affordable for my company to send out a replacement or issue a full refund. This was a cost for which I had to account, as without offering such a service, I wouldn't have received such a healthy Detailed Seller Rating (DSR) and positive feedback, resulting ultimately in customers feeling confident to buy from my eBay shop.

By 1 June 2010, just three months after we started, we were now selling approximately 1,320 items a month, and this rose to 2,091 items in July 2010. By mid-June we had enough money in the business to purchase a laptop exclusively for our work as well as our first additional storage facility – an 8 ft x 6 ft shed that housed our ever-expanding stock levels and took John a day to erect.

We stepped up another gear on 6 July 2010 when we placed our first order with a wholesale supplier who delivered direct to our door.

After hours of trawling the internet, we had stumbled across a supplier in the south-west of England who just happened to sell products similar to some that we were buying direct from the high street, and even better, we could get them up to 40 per cent cheaper. It was a crucial step towards expansion, as not only did it save us money, but also precious time that we so often seemed to lack.

We were now able to browse and order products online from the comfort of our own home, and have the goods delivered to our door. As well as time, this saved money (for petrol, parking, etc.) and eased some of the ever-mounting pressure. I still had to visit the high-street stores, but not nearly as frequently, which was a huge weight off my shoulders.

Up to now my day had consisted of waking up at a ridiculously early hour and getting the kids ready for school, while John went downstairs to print off the day's despatch notes. The first words exchanged between John and I became 'How many today?' instead of the traditional 'Good morning, darling'. Once John had printed off the despatch notes I would have to separate the notes into categories, and then, sometimes in bitter cold and dark conditions, go to the shed in the garden to pick the day's products while the children rattled around inside.

On really productive mornings, I would have the picking done an hour before we left for school, and if my children Kane and Jamie were very keen to earn some extra pocket money, they would sit at our dining table wrapping the easier products for despatch. They even, at their request, got involved with the picking of products, too, but were not so keen to do this on the really cold and dark days.

The school run began at 8.30 a.m., involving two drops, followed by a daily trip to the various discount stores, which usually took about an hour, sometimes more. At about 10.30 I would arrive home and religiously tune into LBC radio, usually during James O'Brien's slot. Each DJ slot lasted three hours and I used to give myself a target to have my wrapping done by the time James O'Brien's show was over. Sometimes, I'd have it done earlier and reward myself with a break, but most of the time my target would be annoyingly accurate and I would finish the wrapping at bang on 1.00 p.m.

My lunches often only consisted of bags of crisps and Twix bars that I had picked up when shopping for stock, with the occasional treat of a homemade sandwich. Very occasionally, I would have a sneaky breakfast date with a friend who would hunt me down at a discount store and insist I come for a coffee at a café in Muswell Hill.

After bagging the packages into huge IKEA bags, I would then settle in front of the computer for the next two hours, spending one hour researching items I had photographed in the stores. In the following hour, between 2 and 3 p.m., I would photograph and list the newly discovered and bought products from the research carried out the day before.

Research involved first making sure the item could sell by checking my competition on eBay. Once I had found an identical or very similar product, I would place it within a subfolder that I called 'Research' in my 'Watching' items. I would then enter a price a little under my competitor's price onto an Excel spreadsheet (you will find a formula and screen print within Part II of this book) that John had developed for me. Once I had entered my potential selling price and all other relevant costs associated with the product, I would be able to determine if there was still enough profit to make it worthwhile selling it. I would include a margin to lose a little more in the event of being undercut. I would then move the product details to a 'To Be Listed' folder and keep it in that subfolder until it was introduced to my shop. Once the listing was live, I would move my competitors item from my 'Research' subfolder to another subfolder called 'Competitors', and if my item stopped selling I would go back to my 'Competitors' folder to see if there had been any movement in my opposition's price.

My general rule was that I would buy five of the product to begin with. If, however, my competitor beat my price, and I could not afford to undercut them again, then I wouldn't be stuck with loads of stock to make a loss on. On the flip side, if my pricing didn't appear threatened, and if my competitor began to steer clear of the product, then I would gradually introduce more of the same line. If the line was particularly good, I would generally try to obtain as many of that item as I could.

I got my listing speed right down from a slow fifteen minutes per listing at the beginning to five minutes or even less if I was listing a 'Sell Similar' product (where the concept of the product was the same, with only the brand being different). In the hour before having to leave on the school run, which I always did by the skin of my teeth, I could usually manage to list approximately eight to ten items, including photography and uploading time. This meant that each day I was adding between five and ten lines to my eBay shop, depending on how successful the research in preceding days had been.

With each new line, I would have to spend more time picking and, more worryingly, wrapping for the next day's despatch. It was getting to a point where I couldn't get the wrapping done in James O'Brien's slot alone, and it was now often spilling over into the 1 p.m. show on LBC. This was leaving me little or even no time to list new products, and so I started to find myself doing my store research and purchasing in the afternoon more often, dragging the kids around with me.

I knew this couldn't work long term. I felt guilty enough that I was involving the children in the post office drop, often leaving them waiting in the truck while I'd unload, so taking them to collect stock as well was just too much. I must say, however, that during this whole period they were impeccably behaved and never seemed phased at all, often distracted by the friendliness of the stores' staff, who really took them under their wings.

Carrying out research in the latter part of my day meant that I was getting home later and later, sometimes after 5 p.m., and the stress was really getting to me. The business was still in its early stages, but the pace was fast and the growth phenomenal. I would take time out to read with the children and cook dinner, but as soon as they were in bed, I would be back at my desk spending hours on the internet looking for suppliers and both cost- and time-saving strategies.

As a precaution for better health, I also took up swimming, and swam every day for thirty minutes. I could be in and out of the pool building within one hour, and I found that it helped clear my mind. As a result, I worked much more effectively, so the time missed while I swam was negligible as the quality of work I began to produce was much better. More importantly, I felt calmer within myself and around my children.

However, eventually my shop just got too busy and I succumbed to the guilt and the pressure, knowing that the only way to keep climbing was to employ help. On 19 July 2010, just four months after starting the business, we employed the services of our friend's daughter Georgia for just one afternoon to help clear a backlog. We decided the fairest way to pay her was by the package and paid approximately 30p per item wrapped. She wrapped sixty-seven items waiting for despatch and earned £20 in just three hours.

I was now completing many of my listings in the evening, and on one night every week, my mum would collect the boys from school and keep them overnight, taking them up to school for me the following morning. This was a huge help and meant that I effectively had eighteen hours of uninterrupted time from when they left in the morning until I collected them the following afternoon. As I adapted to this new routine, I would collect new lines in a bag designated 'Awaiting Listing', and would sometimes list as many as thirty or forty items in these windows of time, which was invaluable, especially as we prepared for the busy season ahead. It also gave me a chance to review my stock levels and tidy up the sometimes very messy shed, and more importantly time to sit and reflect on the growth of the business thus far.

We then enlisted the help of my stepdaughter Lauren, who was thirteen at the time. She came to stay with us and earned the grand total of £150 in just a few afternoons of wrapping, which helped her to have a very good summer indeed. By 27 August 2010, we were sending out in excess of seventy items per day.

Having Lauren there to help take away some of the pressure and time it took for us to wrap gave me the opportunity to expand even further by listing more lines. By the middle of August 2010 we purchased plasterboard and fittings to kit out our bare and disused loft space. John installed a pull-down ladder, insulated and boarded the loft and finished it with a Velux window.

It felt huge compared to our small shed in the garden and expansion was now in sight. It didn't take long at all to fill the loft, especially with Christmas fast approaching. At first, I hated the squeaky and rickety pull-down loft ladder, especially when climbing up or coming down with blue IKEA bags full of heavy stock. It had always been easy taking the stock in and out of the garden shed. With time, however, my confidence grew, although I was never entirely at ease with the ladder despite John's constant reassurance about its strength.

I never realised just how sensible and strong my stepdaughter was until we shared times dragging box after box full of heavy stock up to the loft and then sorting it out in an order where it could be reached. I would always pay Lauren per parcel, but for times when she helped with stock moving, I'd pay her by the hour and she was fast accruing a healthy sum of money.

After a few shopping trips to spend some of her hard-earned cash, and after three weeks with us, Lauren returned to her mum and we then employed the services of another helper. He began working for us on 9 September 2010 and daily after that.

He would arrive really early every morning, sometimes by 7.30 a.m. on a busy day, and he was reliable some of the time. There were mornings, however, when he wouldn't turn up at all and, to make matters worse, he would not even call to let me know. It was at times like this that I would have complete melt-downs. This first non-family employee was great at what he did, but he was trying to hold down two jobs and he was getting really tired, which I completely understood. On his unreliable days, John would usually step in to help me get the products out and order would resume, but it wasn't long before I made a decision to look for an alternative wrapper.

During the half-term break in October 2010, we were getting incredibly busy in the run up to Halloween and Christmas, so Lauren again stepped in to save the day. She also trained our latest recruit, Azad, and a sterling job she did too.

During very stressful times, a flash of happiness would come and leave me rejuvenated and motivated, and one of these occasions came from an eBay member who sent us an email. Impressed by our feedback figures that we had accrued after such a short length of time, he was seeking advice on setting up an online eBay business. He had been working as a civil servant for some time but had become disillusioned with the nine-to-five routine and wanted to work out whether or not there was a profit to be made as a professional eBay seller. We were candid and honest in our response to him and I think it was way back then that I realised we were not only driving ourselves forward but others too. Complete strangers who had just picked up on our success by browsing our eBay shop and subsequent history wanted to know how it was done, and John and I were more than willing to oblige.

The most memorable enquirer for me was a man called Prab from Birmingham, who got in touch in September 2010. I had bought a set of binoculars from him and he had contacted me by phone to inform me that my item had been despatched by special delivery service. He was a thorough and incredibly helpful seller.

Our conversation went on and inevitably, both being eBay sellers, we talked about the highs and lows of trading online.

Prab was selling very high-value items and so his sales were obviously not as great in volume as mine, which, at the time, were all low-value bargain products.

He was trying to build-up his feedback score and was very eager for me to leave him feedback for the binoculars, which I did promptly. By then my own feedback score was at approximately 8,000 after just six months of trading, so he was naturally curious. We spoke at length about my low-cost approach and I explained that, for me, it was more about volume than the actual value of the goods, especially in the economic climate in which we were selling. On the morning that Prab called, my wrapper had let me down and I had heaps to catch up on, so I was feeling a little low and his call definitely lifted my spirits. Let's just say he inspired me that day, probably much more than I inspired him, and he left me thoroughly rejuvenated after our long conversation. We would chat a few more times after that and he picked me up when I was feeling low. He often said that I should keep a blog and he had a lot more belief in me than I ever did in myself. Prab embedded the seed that became this book. Sadly, as the business grew busier and busier, I had hardly any time to devote even to my closest of friends, and Prab and I lost touch.

With more and more packages to wrap and despatch, the transferring of packages from my house to the post office was often taking up, at the very least, an hour of my day. It was always a rush and very stressful, as I would usually tend to do it en route to the school and nursery. The postmistress noticed my anxiety and, at the beginning of summer 2010, she suggested that I should just drop off the packages with her, entrusting her to stamp them and despatch them, with me paying in arrears for the previous day's post. She did this on the condition that I weighed everything and marked the weight on each package prior to it arriving at the post office, so I invested in a set of digital scales. Now, as part of the wrapping process, each item would be weighed and marked in the right-hand corner of each address label. The system worked very well up until October 2010, but by then our truck could no longer hold the amount of packages we were despatching each day (over eighty orders) and two drops just wasn't an option.

It was during this period that we decided to look at other despatch services, much to the disappointment of the postmaster and mistress at our post office who, at the mention of such an idea in the weeks before, had tried strenuously to deter us from taking such a route. I always see the absolute best in people 100 per cent of the time so I suppose I was a little ignorant thinking that here they were doing me a favour out of the goodness of their hearts, letting me drop off my packages, queue jump and pay in arrears. However, as they tried to dissuade me more and more from using another service, the penny dropped and I realised that they too were a profit-making business, and I was bringing a lot their way!

After careful thought and consideration, on 7 October 2010 our exhaustive and very time-consuming trips to the post office ended and we signed a contract with a commercial mailing company. With hindsight, this was the biggest mistake we have made to date! Although it saved us time and money, it was headache after headache trying to deal with a profit-making company which, in my opinion, didn't seem to give a damn about its customer!

At the enquiry stage John had approached the Royal Mail customer service team for me about the level of items we were despatching every day and we were offered advice on various options, one being Packetpost and the other being the franking machine option. During the conversation, wires must have crossed because John came away from the call with the understanding that the mailing company and Packetpost were one company, so we did what we thought was the sensible thing and approached the company direct.

A sales rep arrived at our door some days later. By this stage, as our company was sending out in excess of eighty items per day, both myself and John were a little distracted to say the least, so I had completely forgotten our appointment. I remember it was a Wednesday and I was delayed because I had stupidly gone to my regular post office to do the drop after going to the supermarket, completely forgetting that they closed early on Wednesdays.

If it had been any other time, I would have waited until the next day to do the drop, but I was carrying a particularly high volume of second-class packages for Halloween, and with 31 October just around the corner, the despatch couldn't wait. This meant a trip to another post office and I arrived there just before 5 p.m. when post offices are at their absolute busiest. I wandered in with my herd of packages to despatch and then, very frustratingly, had to wait for the postmaster to reweigh and stamp every single item! He understandably couldn't trust my measurement of weight and, as you can probably imagine, I lost my temper just a little.

I arrived home late with bagfuls of shopping and three hungry boys, and my stress levels were through the roof, especially when I saw a whole load of mess from the day's wrapping!

John introduced me to the sales rep and we spoke about the franking machine service offered. In our ignorance, we kept asking her about Packetpost. We were under the misapprehension that it was an additional service offered by them and she didn't have the paperwork to hand. Believing that Packetpost was an extension of the franking machine service, we naively signed a year's contract in the chaos of our dining room and awaited the arrival of the machine and associated paraphernalia. I was probably not in the best state of mind for such an important meeting, but fate had just played a bad hand that day.

From that point onwards, trying to contact our sales rep was almost impossible and on the few times we did manage to speak she would reassure us that the information on Packetpost was coming. I began to worry about the paperwork we had signed and on further investigation realised that we had in fact tied ourselves into a year's contract with a company who had absolutely nothing at all to do with Packetpost.

Soon we were stuck with a machine that was costing us money to rent from a company we had mistakenly signed up for a year's business and we were very disheartened. We tried to remain upbeat and philosophical. At least the trip to the post office was now a thing of the past, as we had arranged Royal Mail collections directly from our house, and we were saving some money on postage, so we figured it wasn't so bad after all.

We trained Azad on how to use the new franking machine and as the Christmas rush began he brought in his friend Ramz to help. It was now November 2010 and we were pushing out in excess of 100 items a day, and during this period had a daily turnover figure of over £400. Azad and Ramz worked together until we closed for Christmas on 22 December 2010.

With the rush of buyers, I was inevitably purchasing more and more stock from my local discount stores; members of staff within the shops became increasingly curious as did fellow customers. Because I was now working to incredibly tight deadlines, I would often try to avoid the onslaught of questions and after several conversations with Alex and other store managers, we agreed that it was better for everybody if I began ordering my regular stock lines on the telephone.

This worked better for the store managers, too, as they were not always available to deal with my stock demands if I turned up unannounced at random times of the day. The plan was that I would arrive much later in the day to collect, sometimes when the store was about to close. The store managers would gather the stock together for me throughout the day at a time convenient for them and load it on to a trolley to await my arrival. I would arrive and pay at the till with a receipt the manager had already prepared on his office computer (on a system especially designed for bulk orders). Meanwhile, the staff in the store would load my truck through the rear exit.

Coming in and out through the back of the stores, I entered a whole new world. The exit at one of the stores was at the end of a very long and narrow alley with lots of cigarette butts and endless cardboard boxes. Often I would chat with staff having their five-minute cigarette or coffee break and even joined in with an impromptu barbecue they were having one very hot afternoon, using disposable BBQ sets from inside the store! There was even one time when I turned up with the kids straight from school in thick snow and ice, and we all ended up having a snowball fight with Alex!

As you can imagine, the kids loved it, as they did the freebies that Alex would lavish on them from sweets through to small toys. I was even given a very big basket on wheels to fill full of freebies as the Christmas rush approached, by which time I was spending in excess of £1,000 every time I visited the store.

I grew close to Alex and his staff and remember putting them not only on my Christmas card list, but a couple of them on my Christmas gift list too. They were very supportive in my pursuit and helped me in any way they could, ringing me about limited stock lines that were coming in, holding stock back for me, letting me look at idle stock, and even going as far as to invite me to the staff Christmas party. They made me feel like one of them and I appreciated that, especially as eBay trading was, at times, an isolating role to play.

In the run up to Christmas and with such a lot of packages being wrapped, our kitchen/dining room was no longer the hub of our home, but more a workshop where myself, John and the kids were just getting in the way. Azad and Ramz were sometimes working until late into the evening trying to get the ever-mounting orders ready for the postman and inevitably dinner was getting prepared and served later and later every night.

It was during the Christmas break, after this extremely stressful and busy time, that we decided that the business was now too big to continue life inside our home. Rather than reopening as planned at the end of January 2011, we remained closed while we worked out how to reorganise it.

John and I discussed building a huge shed in the garden to capacitate not only more stock lines that I wanted to introduce, but also somewhere Azad and Ramz could work. It had to be large, functional, insulated and, most importantly, cheap to build.

So, in February 2011, during the spring half term, our friend's son Luke came to stay with us for a week to help John dismantle our old shed (which we sold on eBay) and replace it with a building that replicated the drawings John had planned. This equated to a 17 x 13 feet (221 square feet) bespoke wooden building that was designed to suit the thirty-degree slope at the rear of our garden.

It was as big as we could build without planning permission and every inch of space was utilised effectively and precisely. It was insulated from top to bottom and had electricity too. With a little fan heater it was sometimes warmer in there than inside our house, and had been designed so that Azad and Ramz's workstation looked out of two windows on to our garden and beyond on to our house.

It was a great view for them, rather than one confronted by kitchen cabinets like before, but it also meant that John and I could keep an eye on them, making sure that they were working and not chatting away on their phones all day long, which we had to pick them up on more than once.

The entire build was funded by profits from our business and the business was now able to grow even more, which it did, quicker than we could ever have imagined.

As with the loft, it didn't take us long to fill up the new shed, and Ramz and Azad were very excited by their new workspace. The boys were incredibly committed to my ever-expanding business and, I think, had more belief in its growth potential than I ever did. Ramz often remarked that we would 'one day be bigger than ASDA'. Bless him!

We planned to open as springtime approached, so we decided the best way forward was to do a stock take and start the year fresh and accurately. With a lot of help and counting by Azad, Ramz and my oldest friend Phaedra, we were up to date and ready to reopen in March 2011. By the end of March 2011, after two months of being closed, we hit the ground running with 2,072 orders for that month alone.

It was three months later, on 14 June 2011, after many heated telephone conversations with our mailing company, that we eventually managed to get them to see reason and honour the cancellation of our year-long contract, which was now null and void due to the conduct of their sales rep, not to mention the appalling customer service. In fairness, we were compensated for the trouble caused, and we went on to open a Packetpost contract with the Royal Mail, effectively becoming our own postmasters and saving up to 25 per cent on postage charges.

The Royal Mail Packetpost service quite simply turned our lives around and we were delighted. The staff were helpful, factual, supportive and, most importantly, were at the other end of a phone that was actually answered whenever we needed guidance.

We began paying £500 a year, which we would not have to pay after the first year if we spent more than £15,000 per year on postal services (which we did). Even if we hadn't spent that amount in a year with the Royal Mail, the collection service and the substantial savings we made just by using this direct service more than compensated for the charge.

We not only saved ourselves time and money, but more important than any of that was the fact that I didn't have to worry about getting to the post office before it closed anymore or have to find a parking space to unload. Endless queues were a thing of the past, as well as the one thing that used to drive me up the wall the most: the endless tuts, sneers and complaints from the unfortunate customers behind me! I had often queued like everybody else and sometimes had my kids with me, who were waiting in line too after a long day at school, so to hear the tuts in front of them from a person leisurely waiting to post a letter or cash in on a winning scratchcard used to drive me crazy!

Being our own postmasters, we would now stamp, weigh, bag and process everything, and the Royal Mail held our hand throughout the process until we were entirely confident with doing it ourselves. They also supplied us with limitless amounts of the bags, cable ties and other paraphernalia that we needed. Unlike Pitney Bowes, this was all free of charge, as was their helpline.

The products that we wrapped and prepared were collected from our door five days a week at a timeslot to suit us by our lovely postman, Marlon. He was somebody with whom we really built up a relationship, as did our kids as he became a constant part of our daily life.

In the first year of trading our wonderful accountant, Leon, informed me that in year one our postage costs were 35 per cent of overall costs, but by moving over to Packetpost with Royal Mail, in year two (2011–12) we got that cost down to 17 per cent, a massive 50 per cent saving.

When I think of how much money we could have saved in that first year of trading just by knowing about Packetpost, I realise that this sort of inside information alone should make it worthwhile picking up this book and having a nose.

John and I often have heated debates, with me saying eBay selling requires skill whereas he believes this not to be the case. It is true that anyone can sell on eBay, it is true that anyone can do a listing and it is true that anybody can make some money doing so too. However, not everybody is 'anybody' and not 'anybody' can become 'somebody'. There are different levels of sellers selling different levels of stock. To become a fast and successful power-seller requires patience, skill, tenacity, determination and sheer hard work, and with these crucial tools you can truly do anything on eBay.

Do not let eBay use you: you have to use eBay. With our help you can learn the systems and develop a winning formula as professional eBay sellers. For us eBay win and we win too. Our ultimate goal is to earn more out of our business than what eBay makes out of us (which we haven't quite managed yet).

I haven't made it rich yet, but I am steadily on my way there. When I look at the initial sales figures of some of the country's biggest sellers, I can say that my first-year figures exceeded their first-year figures, so I am hopeful for a bright future if I continue on the path I have pursued.

I made approximately 20,000 sales in my first year of trading, having begun in March 2010. On 20 May 2010, after less than two months, I was upgraded to become a Silver Powerseller, and on 18 August, within five months of starting out, I was upgraded again to Gold. On 18 December of that same year, nine months from my very first sale, I was awarded Platinum status.

With each of these upgrades I received discounts from my eBay Final Value Fees which kept pushing up my profit margins. In my first twelve months of trading on eBay I turned over almost £100,000 with a feedback score exceeding 12,000 and sales reaching 20,000.

On the back of our continued success we have inspired ten individual friends (including two friends in New York) and members of my own family, who have now begun to create their very own eBay shops, and with our advice, some have seen their sales figures double almost instantly.

I would love, more than anything, for you to let us help you to do the same with our compact and, I promise, easy to follow guide.

I relocated to Frome in Somerset in February 2012 and, one day in particular, I was visiting a local store that had just opened. While at the till, I began talking with a lovely lady who had just been employed by the new store. She was helping to pack my bags and told me how she had struggled for years trying to find a job. She was about my age, possibly a year or two older, and the delight and pride on her face made me quite emotional. She was just overjoyed that she was working again and paying her way.

We are living in desperate times with people not knowing where to turn and I hope you, the reader, will feel as inspired as my friends and family have and see that there is a way out of the dole queue or the rat race.

I was devastated when I was told that I would not have my temporary contract at the hospital renewed after ten months of working within a department that felt more of a community than a place of work. It was somewhere I thrived and I had established bonds both professionally and personally that would inevitably be broken once I had left the department. To lose a job's sense of belonging and identity and, more importantly, its crucial income can lead to the downfall of many, yet it motivated me to find another direction which I hope will inspire and lead others to find a way out too.

eBay's virtual world can often be a lonely place and with me being such a sociable and gregarious character I am somewhat, ironically, a bit like a fish out of water.

As I mentioned earlier, it was people's curiosity and my fellow eBay trader Prab that sowed the seed for this book when he said that I should keep a blog of my daily antics as a trader, but it was a friend of mine who has successfully written, illustrated and published several children's picture books that got me really thinking about offering an eBay training service. She runs courses for people who are interested in a career in writing books with a view to getting them published and I felt inspired by her work and wondered if training others would be something I could offer too.

When people like my ten friends and family feel inspired to motivate themselves through something I might have said, I really feel as if I am making a difference in their lives. It is this that drives me forward to help others.

Just two months after arriving in Frome, in April 2012, I happened to have a telephone conversation with a local estate agent and he wanted to know where I was from and what I was looking for. This inevitably led to me telling him that I had relocated to Frome to expand my eBay business.

A few days later I went to meet him for a prearranged viewing of a property he had for sale in Frome, where we resumed our eBay conversation. His wife was very interested in opening an eBay shop herself and had been struggling to make a go of it so I casually gave him my number and told him I was happy to help her along. Within a few days of that meeting, Leah got in touch and she visited me for a very informal training session on eBay trading. The upcoming school summer holidays and an unexpected relocation within Frome put Leah's training on hold. My plan, however, is to now develop a course, initially for local people, using Leah as my guinea pig. I have promised her continued free mentoring in exchange for constructive criticism and guidance both on my teaching approach and that of my book, and she has been more than happy to oblige.

For me to teach others the skills of eBay will take me back where I belong, working with other people, and it is here that I know I can thrive, by bouncing off other people and their journeys.

So far I have very casually mentored just a few people, but to see the excitement in their eyes is really motivating and my pride in those that are now starting to succeed is overwhelming.

Even my stepdaughter Lauren now wants to get involved on a bigger scale. She is a teenager struggling to find work and, like all young girls, wants the nice things money can bring. We are setting her up with a shop of her own and, with us behind her, we are sure that she will succeed.

On eBay the buyer-to-seller ratio is approximately 20/1, with 200 million buyers worldwide accessible to each and every one of us. As sellers we are drowning in buyers and there is a department within the eBay network to suit sellers in any category within which they wish to specialise.

We have attempted to keep this guide short and to the point. We accept that the majority of people who pick up this book will have a little common sense, so we are really just skimming the surface for you.

You, the reader, have your own skills and your own desire for what you wish to sell, and we are just equipping you with the necessary tools to start you off.

I can't promise that it will be easy, but if you want a job that allows you to be home-based and flexible, then this can be an option for you.

There will be mountains of work at the beginning, even for as long as the first two years, but gradually, as you will see from the 'Diary Days' section below, it really does begin to get easier.

Do not be fooled by those who tell you it is easy. It isn't. It gets easy, but the beginning, as with anything in life, has to be endured.

When learning how to drive, you are taught over a period of time, sometimes weeks or even months. If you follow the instructions, the car will move for you and take you to places you may never have seen before. If you drive correctly, you will be rewarded with a licence to go to those unfound places. If not, you will fail and may never get back in the driving seat again. Some will give up, but others will keep on trying, and this guide is for the ones who keep trying, and who will eventually reap the ultimate rewards that eBay can bring.

eBay, like a car, is a tool that needs to be used precisely and accurately. It is a formula of rules and regulations, and they are absolute. You may get lucky by not following a systematic approach, but in the end luck always eventually runs out. If you want consistent success you must follow the route supplied to get you to the right place.

John and I had no one to guide us, and we spent a long time making mistakes. It was only through meeting the right people, having the right conversations and making those many mistakes that we found an easier way and instructed ourselves accordingly. Perhaps we had a skill, perhaps we didn't. We can only go by our figures and feedback ratings, and, so far, they tell us we are doing OK.

In the 'Diary Days' section you will see entries documenting the very beginning of our journey and a more recent day in 2011. I have done this to illustrate that as much as it is very gruelling at the beginning, there is light at the end of the tunnel and you do begin to reap the rewards of the hard work you put in if you just hang on in there.

In the first 'Diary Days' section, you will see that I was working sometimes more than fifteen hours a day, seven days a week, but now my week is much more leisurely and my day is generally wrapped up by 4.30 p.m.

Once you have an established and flourishing eBay business in place, you can choose to live anywhere you like and will no longer be governed by rail networks and good road links. You will be your own boss who sets and reaches your own targets at your own pace, and before long you too will have a team that work for you.

We now add new products at our leisure as the lines we are running are enough for the time being to support our family comfortably. As mentioned earlier, the only thing holding us back is space.

We no longer have a post office run to do as the Royal Mail collect from our door, and we can turn our shop on and off as we please if we need a break to do things like writing this book or to go on holiday. Our weekends are our own and we do not work at all during these times.

Our children have become more and more involved with the business and now often volunteer themselves for wrapping to raise extra pocket money while finding a strong work ethic, i.e. that work equals money, a message we like to encourage.

We have been able to show them that if you put your mind to it, and with very little outlay, you can turn a broom cupboard into a double garage full of stock by working hard and following just a few simple rules.

My proudest moment to date was in July 2011 when I got an email from the BBC inviting me for an audition for *The Apprentice*. I was naturally nervous when I had to stand in front of three programme producers and eleven fellow applicants to explain why I thought I was the next Apprentice.

My nerves definitely got the better of me that day, but I somehow managed to get through the process and was subsequently ushered upstairs to have a one-to-one chat with a programme researcher. This was a much more relaxed experience and we spoke at length about my seventeen-month-old eBay business. There were a lot of memorable moments during that process, but the comment that stayed with me and made me beam with pride was when the researcher called my story 'an inspiration'.

I left that room with my head in the clouds and the sun on my face and, although I never got called back to be on the programme, that comment alone was confirmation enough for me that I didn't need a television show to get me to where I needed to go. I now had the confidence I needed to step up with my business and to begin to make a difference.

eBay is just a formula, and even my eight- and twelve-year-old boys and my fifteen-year-old daughter, who have been part of our eBay business for the past two years, now understand perfectly how to make something sell, and so can you.

Happy eBaying and let your journey to success begin. I will not wish you luck, because it isn't about luck. Just follow the steps, stand strong, stay determined and you will succeed.

DIARY DAYS

15 MARCH 2010

Consignments to despatch: 25

This is one of my typical days as an inexperienced eBay trader before any of my systems were in place. At this point I was still holding down a day job at the hospital.

06:45   Up to get myself and the boys ready while John prints off a summary of sales as my guide for picking and reference point for addressing labels/envelopes.

07:30   I breakfast and finish off getting boys ready, then go and get the products that need to be wrapped that morning.

07:45   John helps me to wrap the products in black bin-liners. My son Kane likes to get involved so helps stuff a few envelope-worthy products at the dining table.

08:00   Boys are all ready. We begin hand-writing labels and envelopes. John and I finish off the products for the day while the boys watch TV before the school run.

08:30   John, myself and the boys leave for work/school with the packages stored in an IKEA bag in the boot of my car ready for me to take to the post office after work at the hospital today.

13:00 During my lunch hour at work I start researching stock and stumble across and review an auction-style website selling graded used and unused customer returns. I also have a chance to answer some eBay customer queries.

15:00 Leave work and collect boys from school and nursery.

15:30 Arrive at the post office. All stock dropped off and paid for. Postmistress says black bags are splitting, as are the envelopes we are using!

16:00 Arrive home with the boys. I grab them both a snack and they watch television while I get on with tidying up the mess made from this morning's wrapping.

16:15 Begin listing items on 'Auction' and 'Buy It Now' and answer the remaining questions that have come in since lunchtime today. Not many … we are still on a pretty small scale.

17:00 John arrives home and we start dinner.

19:30 Get kids bathed, story time, tucked in and asleep.

20:00 Back downstairs to continue research of products. Takes hours!

23:00 Computer off … Chat with John about sourcing new packaging materials, watch a little TV and then off to bed.

2 JUNE 2011

Consignments to despatch: 80

I am now a much more experienced eBay trader and employ the services of a picker and packer. We have a contract with Royal Mail, which collects from us daily.

07:00 John and I wake up and while I get on with getting the boys ready for school John prints the despatch notes. He then begins to answer the maximum amount of ten estions from our buyers and then hands over the despatch notes to our picker and packer.

08. I put the despatch notes in order of product and then divide them into two piles ... one for the loft and one for the shed (this is something our wrappers eventually begin to do for themselves).

08:30 I take the boys to school and pick up any personal shopping and/or stock.

09:30 Home! Check on Azad and/or Ramz and help them out with any queries/problems.

10:00 I now update stock levels and list any new items. No more wrapping for me. Now that I have discovered Turbo Lister rather than the traditional eBay listing method, each listing is now taking me as little as three minutes to complete.

11:00 John takes the photographs of our new lines and uploads them on to Photobucket before transferring them on to our scheduled listings waiting to go live.

14:30 John leaves to collect the boys from school and nursery and I get on with preparing dinner.

15:30 John returns home to begin the processing of the post. This takes approximately thirty minutes. The post is sorted into categories by our picker and packer, and then handed to John, who weighs it, enters the details on to the online account with Royal Mail and labels the bags. Royal Mail collects from our door at 5 p.m. Our day's work is done.

After a year of learning and adopting new systems we have increased sales by as much as 367 per cent and, as you can see, we now save ourselves a ton of time.

We no longer work late into the evening. Our day starts at 7 a.m. and finishes by 5 p.m. at the very latest, and this is by no means an exhausting day's work.

The automated systems that we have put in place now pick up the huge bulk of the work and we are there to oversee the sales, post and stock levels, adding new lines and growing our business to achieve a higher turnover and net profit.

Whereas before our day was non-stop from 7 a.m. until sometimes 10 or 11 p.m. every night seven days a week, we now have a life and more importantly are generating an income in what seems to be a profitable business.

We have high stock levels that we have built up over the past two years and we employ the services of a picker and packer. On quieter days/weeks we still pack ourselves, but during busier periods our wrappers are there and play an integral part in helping our business grow. Having our wrappers gives John and I the opportunity to do the crucial research needed to add more stock lines and get them live in our shops.

For every new product we add, we generate more income. The eBay fees are high, so driving those costs down is something we strive for every day to increase our net profits, with a little bit of help from our wonderful accountant, Leon Perkin, and our amazing bookkeeper, Sue Levy.

FACTS AND FIGURES

MONTHLY SALES APRIL 2010–MAY 2011

	Sales	Approx. Daily	Repeat Custom	Turnover Figures
Apr 2010	627	21	–	£2,700
May 2010	1480	48	–	£6,364
Jun 2010	1324	44	5.5%	£5,701
Jul 2010	2091	67	5.7%	£8,032
Aug 2010	2202	71	7.9%	£8,573
Sept 2010	2200	73	8.5%	£8,274
Oct 2010	2536	81	8.2%	£9,650
Nov 2010	3079	102	9.4%	£12,091
Dec 2010	1848	59	7.3%	£7,570
Jan 2011	CLOSED			
Feb 2011	CLOSED			
Mar 2011	2072	66	6.6%	£8,239
April 2011	2693	89	6.7%	£11,297
May 2011	2557	82	5.4%	£11,446

The above figures are a breakdown of my total gross revenue starting from zero at the beginning of April 2010. As you can see, my eBay business took £99,937 in sales during a twelve-month period of online trading. The shop remained closed for the period between January and February 2011 inclusive while we built our external workshop in the garden.

PART II

Starting Your Own eBay Business

2
RESEARCHING THE MARKET

DECIDING WHAT TO SELL

Deciding what you are going to sell is essential to creating a successful business. We recommend that you initially sell in a category with which you are familiar. For example, if you have experience as a hairdresser, you might want to think about selling hair products and/or hairdressing equipment, or if you are a carpet fitter you may want to sell carpets/underlay and fitting equipment/tools relating to that industry.

INTERESTS AND HOBBIES

If you have a keen interest or hobby it is worthwhile applying your acquired knowledge to your business.

Approaching your business in this way gives you the opportunity to start with a good knowledge of the products you have chosen to sell. You will probably be familiar with the products and brands associated with your chosen category, and you will be able to make informed decisions when deciding what to purchase. You may even already know some wholesalers or importers and will have the benefit of being able accurately to describe the items to your potential purchasers. This will enable you to answer quickly and effectively any queries they may have regarding the products and even provide them with advice or recommendations.

 Tip

When selling fragile items bear in mind the limitations of our postal system – if you send fragile items expect to get damages.

UNFAMILIAR CATEGORIES

If you choose to sell in a category with which you are unfamiliar, you must be prepared to research thoroughly the products you are intending to sell. You need to describe the item accurately, know its limitations and benefits, and be able to answer any queries your potential buyer may have. You need to be able to sort the value-for-money budget items from the low-quality cheap items, and the quality, trusted brands from the overpriced pretenders. You need to know where your item sits in the marketplace and market it accordingly.

eBay Pulse (http://pulse.ebay.co.uk) is a useful tool to assist you in deciding what you should sell. Here you can find the top searches, top sellers, largest shops and most watched items overall, broken down by category.

Got an idea? Let's see if it works …

 Tip

Choose to sell in a category that is familiar to you or you have a keen interest in – you will already have a knowledge of the items you are intending to sell.

RESEARCHING YOUR ITEMS

Now you have established what you are going to sell, you need to ensure that it will sell, and more importantly, that it will sell at a profit.

STARTING YOUR RESEARCH

The best place to start is eBay itself. Use the search facility to find the item you want to sell; search for 'buy it now' only. It is very rare for an auctioned item to exceed the purchase price of one being offered for sale as 'buy it now'. Make a note of the selling price of the item and the quantity that has sold. By clicking on the 'quantity sold' link you will be able to see when and for how much each one sold. Add the item to your watch list in eBay for future reference. Having a competitor's listing for comparison will be of great assistance when it comes to compiling your own listing.

If you can purchase the item for less than it is retailing on eBay then it is likely you are able to make money.

It is a worthwhile exercise to create a number of watching folders relating to different categories or product groups and placing your watched items into the relevant folder. This will make it easier for you to locate the items for reference at a later date.

Tip

Look out for small items that can be despatched as a letter – your P&P will be cheap and storage space will be maximised.

CAN YOU MAKE MONEY?

The next step is to compile a table or spreadsheet with nine columns with the following headings: Item, Purchase Price, Sale Price, P&P Charged, P&P Cost, eBay Fee, PayPal Fee, Profit, % Return

This can be done on a piece of paper with a calculator, but it is much more efficient to use a spreadsheet package such as Microsoft Excel. The formulae are provided below and will calculate the totals for you automatically.

A sample spreadsheet is available for free download from: http://www.4shared.com/office/ieuu4EDr/Ebay_Calculator.html.

Under each heading enter the relevant information:

Item – Enter each item name or description

Purchase Price – Enter the price at which you can purchase the item

Sale Price – Enter the price at which you can sell the item

P&P Charged – If the item is selling with free P&P leave this field blank or enter the P&P value quoted on your researched listing

P&P Cost – There will always be a P&P cost (unless the item is being sold as collection only) so enter the cost you expect to pay for postage and packaging of the item into the 'P&P Cost' column. Don't be tempted to ignore your packaging costs because this takes time as well as materials

eBay Fee – For each sale that is made through eBay, eBay will charge a Final Value Fee. Dependant on the category in which you have chosen to sell, this will vary, but it is usually 10 per cent of the sale price. If you are intending to list a large quantity of each item on each listing the listing fee becomes negligible, but if you are selling only one item per listing factor this cost into your calculation (usually £0.10 to £0.20 for a basic listing).

Excel formula: =C2*10%

PayPal Fee – For each payment received via PayPal you will be charged £0.20 + 3.4% of the value of the transaction. This percentage will reduce if you register as a business and conduct a certain number or value of transactions within a set period. A £10 transaction will cost you £0.54

Excel formula: =(B2+C2)*3.4%+0.2

Profit – To work out your profit on each sale add the Sale Price to the P&P Charged then subtract the Purchase Price, P&P Cost, eBay Fee and PayPal Fee

Excel formula: =(B2+C2)-D2-E2-F2-A2

% Return – To calculate the percentage return add the Sale Price to the P&P Charged then divide by the Profit, make a note of the value and divide 100 by it. This figure will tell you what percentage of your turnover is profit

Excel formula: =1/((B2+C2)/G2)

👍 **Tip**

Buy a maximum of five items of a new product – test it out and, if it sells, buy more. If it doesn't, you only have five to get rid of.

COMPETITION

It is very important to ascertain that there is a healthy profit. Competition on eBay is fierce, and if you start selling a product cheaper than the competition the likelihood is that they will respond by undercutting you in return. You don't want to be stuck with large sums of money invested in unprofitable or unsellable stock because your competition undercut you and you can't afford to reduce your prices further.

Time spent at the research stage will be rewarded as you progress. Be sure that you consider the saleability of the item; it is important to invest in the faster selling items initially so that you can get a quick turnover to generate more cash for further investment.

Now that you've worked out which items sell and you have a visual confirmation that your items are profitable, it is time to negotiate with your supplier in an attempt to increase that profit margin and percentage return on your investment. Larger orders will be rewarded with larger discounts, but keep your initial order sensible.

SOURCING YOUR STOCK

Unless you are very lucky and already have access to a wholesaler this part of your research will probably be the most time consuming. It requires a tenacious attitude and hours of intensive research on the internet.

SOURCES OF INFORMATION

If you know the manufacturer of the item, ask them to supply the distributor's details – they are always keen to do this. The distributor will probably be happy to pass on the contact details for local wholesalers. It is very unlikely that the retail outlet will reveal their source, but if you don't ask, you don't get. Sometimes you will get lucky and the high-street suppliers will leave the wholesalers', distributors' or importers' information on the item, packaging or packing carton, so be sure to keep your eyes open when browsing local stores.

FAIRS

The Spring and Autumn Fairs at the Birmingham NEC showcase the goods of many wholesalers. You will get the opportunity to meet them and browse the products on offer. Hopefully you should leave with some firm contacts.

👍 **Tip**

Keep your eyes peeled for clues to wholesalers and distributors when you are out shopping.

DISCOUNTS

You will often find that the cheaper the source, the higher the minimum order price will be. It will often be the case that the cheaper suppliers are much bigger companies so their minimum spend is far greater than a smaller, family-run establishment.

NEGOTIATE

Once you have found a supplier, don't be afraid to negotiate prices. They are as keen to sell as you are to buy and in some cases the phrase 'if you don't ask you don't get' has never been truer.

CLEARANCE LINES

Suppliers often have large quantities of a product that is end of line/season and they want to clear it to make space for more current stock. Every penny you save equals more profit, so the harder you drive down the cost, the more money you will make.

We recommend that you start with items purchased from the high street, a cash and carry or a wholesaler to get a feel for what sells before approaching distributors and importers. This will give you an opportunity to buy in low volume, get a feel for the market you are moving into and also build a float to spend when you eventually move on to purchasing larger quantities.

👍**Tip**

Add categories to your 'Watching' folders and watch your competition – refer back to them when devising or revising your listing.

3
GETTING STARTED

PREPARING TO DO BUSINESS

In order to set up your eBay business you may need to purchase some equipment. You will need to register with some websites, open accounts and download a few applications. These are all listed below with a brief description. In-depth advice relating to each website or application is included later in this chapter.

EQUIPMENT REQUIRED

Office

Essential: PC or laptop, printer, telephone, digital camera, tape measure, selection of box files, copier paper

Advantageous: smartphone, laser printer, dedicated work area, A4 single integrated label stock

Packing

Essential: Stanley/craft knife, heavy-duty scissors, one-inch tape dispenser, weighing scales, packaging supplies

Advantageous: dedicated packing area, two-inch tape dispenser

---

👍 **Tip**

If possible, keep a computer exclusively for eBay work – it will stay faster for longer and you will have easy access to everything you need.

BRANDING AND LOGOS

It is worthwhile developing a brand identity for your business. Try to decide on a colour scheme that you could use throughout your business. For certain types of business some colours work better than others, so choose carefully. You may get a better idea if you leave this decision until you create your eBay shop as there are several presets to choose from which should simplify matters.

If you do not already have a logo for your business there is a useful free tool at: http://www.eshopbooster.co.uk/logomaker.php.

This tool will create your logo at the correct size for eBay (310 x 90 pixels), with a choice of fonts, backgrounds and special effects.

ACCOUNTS AND DOWNLOADS

The first thing you will need is an email address. We recommend that you set up a webmail account with one of the reputable companies like Gmail, Outlook or Yahoo. Use this email to register your accounts and use it as a catch-all for the thousands of notification emails you will receive from PayPal and eBay. Don't be tempted to use your home email account: you will soon get annoyed with the amount of email you receive.

> 👍 **Tip**
> Devise a brand for your business – it will appear more professional and buyers will trust you more.

PAYPAL

PayPal is the eBay-recommended payment method: it is quick, safe and simple. In order to trade successfully on eBay a PayPal account is a requirement. Registration is simple. All you need is a current bank account, and you are able to send and receive money as soon as the account is opened.

Please refer to the 'Using PayPal' section later in this chapter for further information.

eBAY

This is where it all begins. It is very easy to register a buyer's account: simply fill out an online submission form and you're ready to go. If you already have an eBay buyer's account, you will probably have a very good feedback rating and a feedback score of some description: this is a valuable asset.

Please refer to the 'Opening a Seller's Account on eBay' section later in this chapter for more information.

> 👍 **Tip**
> Orders for Christmas and Halloween items can start as early as August – maximise your seasonal sales by preparing early.

eBAY SHOP

In order to open an eBay shop you need a feedback rating of at least 10 (this is where your old buying account comes in useful) or a verified PayPal account. It is worthwhile setting up a shop as soon as possible after registration. It says to potential buyers, 'I am a serious and committed seller', and if you have a relatively low feedback score it will provide them with some reassurance that you are taking things seriously. Having an eBay shop also brings benefits such as discounted listing fees and search-result ranking boosts.

Please refer to the 'Opening an eBay Shop' section later in this chapter for further information.

SELLING MANAGER PRO

If you are serious about starting a business selling on eBay it is worthwhile signing up for Selling Manager Pro (SMP) immediately so that you can become accustomed to the systems provided by the software. Simply search for 'selling manager pro' in the eBay help pages and subscribe to the service.

Please refer to the 'Using Selling Manager Pro' section later in this chapter for further information.

TURBO LISTER

Turbo Lister is a free download that makes listing your items much simpler than using the eBay listing tool. The benefits that this software delivers are numerous and it is a must-have listing tool. It will speed up the process and is a worthwhile immediate download for any eBay seller.

Don't waste your time using the eBay tool: this will do it better and faster. Simply search for 'Turbo Lister' in the eBay help pages and download the application.

Please refer to the 'Using Turbo Lister' section later in this chapter for further information.

PHOTOBUCKET

Photobucket is a secure online photo-hosting website. It has tools to edit and enhance your photos, and provides the code to enable you to insert photos into your item listing description. It is very easy to create an account and is essential to saving you money by reducing the costs of your listing fees. Extra photos mean extra fees in many eBay categories. Adding photos to your listing description will also provide a professional appearance to your listings.

Please refer to the 'Using Photobucket' section later in this chapter for more information.

AUCTIVA

Auctiva is an online eBay management tool. It will do just about anything you could possibly require from an eBay management tool, but is primarily used by eBay sellers for its cross-promotional tools. It is free and will promote your other items on each of your listings. Also, it is very easy to set up and is fully customisable.

Please refer to the 'Using Auctiva' section later in this chapter for more information.

ROYAL MAIL ONLINE BUSINESS ACCOUNT (RMOBA)

This is the best and cheapest way to send letters and small parcels within the UK. You will make substantial savings in both time and money by setting up an account with the Royal Mail. You can also arrange for the Royal Mail to collect from you on a daily basis for a relatively small fee.

Please refer to the 'Setting Up a Royal Mail Online Business Account' section later in this chapter for more information.

👍 **Tip**

Compare the Royal Mail's prices with those of couriers – sometimes it pays to opt out and send by courier instead.

PARCEL2GO

Parcel2Go is probably the cheapest and most reliable way to employ the services of a courier currently available. With several different carriers and service levels to choose from, they will have an option to suit your requirements.

Please refer to the 'Registering with Parcel2Go' section later in this chapter for more information.

👍 **Tip**

Always put a compliment slip in with your item, thanking the buyer for their custom and giving details to contact if there is any problem. This shows the buyer that you are approachable and often encourages those who have a negative experience to contact you before jumping in and giving you a bad rating or negative feedback.

USING PAYPAL

www.paypal.com

Sign up with the eBay-recommended payment method in order to trade on eBay.

PAYPAL REGISTRATION

Follow the steps below:

1. Type the web address www.paypal.com into your browser
2. Click on the 'Sign Up' link
3. If you already have a business bank account you can immediately register for a business account with PayPal. If you are intending to use your personal bank account you will need to register a private account then upgrade this to a business account later in the registration process. Click the 'Get Started' button in the relevant area
4. Complete the forms and open an account

The account will initially have spending and receiving limits. You will need to get 'verified' and have your sending and receiving limits lifted. It is imperative that these limits are lifted as soon as possible after you create your account. The process can take a few days so start the ball rolling immediately. You do not want to reach your limits and have to stop trading while they are lifted.

Help and advice, and telephone assistance regarding these processes, are available through the help pages.

REPORTS

PayPal offer two different types of report that are useful to eBay businesses. These are the 'Monthly Financial Summary' and 'Monthly Sales Report', and are available to download in a variety of formats or print direct from the website. They will contain a vast amount of usable information for bookkeeping and accounting purposes.

Access the reports by:

1. From the main 'Overview' page, roll your mouse over the 'History' tab
2. Click the 'Reports' link in the dropdown menu
3. Select the type of report you wish to print or view by clicking on the relevant link
4. Select the month or enter the date range you are interested in
5. Click the 'View Report' button
6. View, print or download the page as required

👍 **Tip**

Don't accept cheques – there are too many delays and too many fraudsters.

MICROPAYMENTS

https://micropayments.paypal-labs.com

If you receive large numbers of small payments it may be more cost effective for you to sign up for a PayPal Micropayment account at the above web address. A standard account will currently charge you 3.4 per cent + 20p per transaction, whereas a micro-payment account will charge you 5 per cent + 5p per transaction.

Currently, you will need to set up a separate micropayment account with PayPal to accept payments at this rate. You can apply this account to your low-value items, and apply the standard account to your higher value items.

The threshold for payments to be more profitable under the micropayment scheme is currently £9.38. Even though your product may be under this amount, consider that when buyers make multiple purchases, the micropayment rate may end up costing you more overall. It is a balancing act, and you should weigh up the options carefully.

Tip

Micropayments with PayPal may work for you if you are accepting large numbers of small payments.

OPENING A SELLER'S ACCOUNT ON eBAY

www.ebay.co.uk

REGISTERING A BUSINESS ACCOUNT

If you are new to eBay and do not yet have an account, or want to retain your private account, you will need to register a new business account by following the steps below:

1. Type www.ebay.co.uk into your browser
2. Click on the 'register' link
3. Click the link at the top of the page to register a 'business account'
4. Complete the forms and open an account

CHANGING YOUR EXISTING BUYER'S ACCOUNT TO A SELLER'S ACCOUNT

If you have an existing active buyer's account and have never made a sale on eBay before, the first step is to convert this account to a seller's account.

In order to change your buyer's account to a seller's account all you are required to do is list an item for sale. This can be done free

of charge by compiling a test listing in the category: Everything
Else>Test Auctions>eBay UK Tests – DO NOT BID.

1. Sign in to your eBay account
2. Roll your mouse over the 'Sell' tab in the top right-hand corner of the page
3. Click the 'Sell an item' link
4. Click the link to 'Browse categories'
5. Scroll to the bottom of the menu and click 'Everything Else >'
6. In the next menu click 'Test Auctions >'
7. In the next menu click 'eBay UK Tests – DO NOT BID'
8. Click the 'Continue' button
9. Select 'No' from the pop-up window offering for you to list a variation
10. Click the 'Continue' button
11. Enter a title for your test auction
12. Don't enter a subtitle or the listing will cost you money
13. Type something into the description field
14. Enter a starting price of £0.99p
15. Scroll down to the P&P section and select 'No Postage: Collection in person only' from the dropdown menu
16. Click the 'Continue' button
17. Scroll to the bottom of the page
18. Click the 'List your item' button

eBay will then require that you perform a few tasks to ensure the
validity of your account: simply follow the onscreen prompts.

 Tip
Try to give your business a name that is relevant to your category,
e.g. Stan's Pet Supplies, to boost search-engine results.

CHANGING YOUR PRIVATE ACCOUNT
TO A BUSINESS ACCOUNT

If you have an active seller's account (i.e. you have sold on eBay privately before or have just changed your buyer's account to a seller's account) your next step is to change your private account to a business account:

1. Click the 'My eBay' link at the top right of the page
2. Roll your mouse over the 'Account' tab
3. Click on 'Personal Information' in the dropdown menu
4. Under the subheading 'User ID and Password information' click the 'edit' link next to 'Private Account'
5. Select to change to a business account
6. Proceed through the verification process

ACCOUNT RESTRICTIONS

If you're a new seller, eBay places some restrictions on what, and how much, you can sell. Once you've been a seller for over ninety days, have a proven track record for providing a consistent level of customer service, and are adhering to the eBay rules and policies, these restrictions will be removed from your account. The limits are removed automatically after your selling account has been active for ninety days: you don't need to do anything else.

There may also be restrictions applied to certain 'high risk' item categories so it is worthwhile reading through the eBay help pages if you are considering targeting your business at these areas:

Mobile & Home Phones > Mobile & Smart Phones
Clothing, Shoes & Accessories > Men's Accessories > Sunglasses

Clothing, Shoes & Accessories > Wedding Clothing > Bride

Clothing, Shoes & Accessories > Wedding Clothing > Bridesmaids dresses

Clothes, Shoes & Accessories > Women's Bags

Clothes, Shoes & Accessories > Women's Accessories > Sunglasses

Clothes, Shoes & Accessories > Women's Accessories > Wallets & Purses

Computing >Apple Computers & Components > Apple Desktops

Computing >Apple Computers & Components > Apple Laptops

Computing > Desktop PCs & Monitors > Desktop PCs

Computing > Laptops & Netbooks

Computing > Software

Computing > PC Components > Drives & Storage > USB/ Pen/ Key/ Flash Drives

Consumer Electronics > DVD & Home Cinema

Consumer Electronics > GPS > GPS Systems

Consumer Electronics > MP3 Players

Consumer Electronics > Televisions

Photography > Camcorders

Photography > Digital Cameras

Video Games > Games

Video Games > Consoles

SETTING UP PREFERENCES
FOR YOUR BUSINESS ACCOUNT

To set up your preferences for your eBay business account, follow the steps below:

1. Open eBay
2. Roll your mouse over the 'Account' tab
3. Click 'Site Preferences'

4. Under the heading 'Seller Preferences' locate 'Payment from Buyers'
5. Click 'Show' and 'Edit'
6. Check the checkboxes for the PayPal options
7. Uncheck the box that allows buyers to edit their totals
8. Enter the address you would like non PayPal payments directed to
9. Check the box to 'Always use this payment address, etc'
10. Click the 'Submit' button
11. Use your browser's back button to return to the 'Site Preferences' page
12. Scroll down the page to 'Logos and Branding'
13. Click 'Manage communications with buyers'. This allows you to add personal messages to the automated emails that eBay sends on your behalf
14. Roll your mouse over the email to which you wish to add a message and click the 'add a message' link (see 'eBay customisable texts' at the end of this section for message examples)
15. Scroll down the page and edit your FAQs (frequently asked questions). This is a very useful option as you can answer buyer's questions without them ever having the need to contact you. It is worthwhile taking the time to edit these Q&As as it will save you time in the long run by negating the need to repeatedly answer the same questions posed by different buyers (see 'eBay customisable texts' at the end of this section for message examples)
16. Use your browser's back button to return to the 'Site Preferences' page
17. Scroll down to 'Buyer Requirements'
18. Click 'Show' and 'Edit'

19. Check the checkboxes and adjust the settings to suit your requirements. Don't be tempted to set them to the highest settings: many people have unpaid item strikes or blemishes on their account through no fault of their own. Keep the restrictions sensible and allow the blocked bidders to contact you. They will often explain the reasons they have been blocked and you can make a judgement to allow them to purchase from you despite their account status if you choose
20. Click the 'Submit' button
21. Use your browser's back button to return to the 'Site Preferences' page
22. Scroll down to 'Business Selling preferences'
23. Click 'Show'
24. Beside 'Business seller information on the View item page' click the 'Edit' link
25. Scroll down the page and edit your returns policy and terms and conditions of sale (see 'eBay customisable texts' at the end of this section for message examples)

eBay is now set up ready for use.

✋Tip

Don't let eBay talk you in to offering a free P&P service – it ups eBay's fees and reduces your profit margin so choose wisely.

---

eBAY CUSTOMISABLE TEXTS

Below are examples of texts that can be inserted into the custom-isable areas of the forms completed in the 'Setting up preferences for your business account' section above. It is the reader's respon-sibility to check that the information, policies and terms and conditions they provide on their account comply with the law and eBay's policies.

Step 14 above: communications with buyers

1. **Buyer wins auction**

    Dear Customer, Many thanks for your order, we appreciate your business. If you require any assistance please do not hesitate to contact us through the eBay messaging system, we are very happy to help in any way we can.

2. **Buyer checks out**

    Dear Customer, Many thanks for completing your purchase with us. If your payment was sent before 2 p.m. (Mon–Fri) we promise to despatch your item on the same day, if not it will be despatched on the next available working day. Please do not hesitate to contact us at any time through the eBay messaging system if you have any questions or queries, we are very happy to offer assistance in any way we can.

3. **Order is updated with P&P information**

    Dear Customer, Your purchase is being picked and packed. If your purchase was completed before 2 p.m. (Mon–Fri) your item will be despatched SAME DAY; if your purchase was completed after this time your item will be despatched NEXT WORKING DAY, and you should be receiving your item shortly.

    Depending on the service level of despatch chosen at the time of purchase you should usually expect:

    Economy (2nd Class) items to arrive within 2–3 days from the date of despatch (although Royal Mail does not guarantee this, and the item may take up to 15 working days to arrive).

    Standard (1st Class) items to arrive within 1–2 days from the date of despatch (although Royal Mail does not guarantee this, and the item may take up to 5 working days to arrive).

Get It Fast (Royal Mail Special Delivery) items are guaranteed by Royal Mail to arrive within 24 hours of the date of despatch.

Courier items are usually sent on a 3–5 day service.

If you have any questions or queries please do not hesitate to contact us through the eBay messaging system. We are very happy to offer assistance in any way we can, and guarantee a response within 24 hours.

👍 Tip

Be patient – only consider selling to the world when you feel comfortable with your systems.

Step 15 above: FAQs

1. Postage

Do you post to countries outside the UK?
No, at present we do not post to any countries outside the UK.

How long will it take to process my order?
We can process your order extremely quickly. If you complete your purchase before 2 p.m. (Mon–Fri) your order will be despatched that same day; any purchases completed after 2 p.m. will be despatched on the next working day.

How long will it take to get my item?
We offer 3 service levels that suit most customers' needs: Economy (2nd Class Post) 2–3 day service (may take up to 14 days); Standard (1st Class Post) 1–2 day service (may take up to 5 days); Get It Fast (Special Delivery) guaranteed next working day service. Please see the Royal Mail website for more information regarding these services.

Where do you post from?
We are Royal Mail PPI Account holders and Franking licence holders. All of our picking, packing and despatch is processed from

our premises in ***INSERT LOCATION***. The Royal Mail collects from us on a daily basis and we use different courier services depending on the service level required.

What postal services do you use?
We are Royal Mail PPI account holders and Franking licence holders, so the entire range of Royal Mail services is at our disposal. We also employ the services of a variety of couriers for heavy or bulky items.

I chose 2nd Class Post, where is my item?
2nd Class Post can take up to 14 working days to arrive. If this period has passed and your item still has not arrived, please check with your local sorting office; undeliverable items are returned there for a variety of reasons and postal delivery workers do not always leave a note. If you have any further questions please contact us, we are pleased to help.

I chose 1st Class Post, where is my item?
1st Class Post can take up to 5 working days to arrive. If this period has passed and your item still has not arrived, please check with your local sorting office; undeliverable items are returned there for a variety of reasons and postal delivery workers do not always leave a note. If you have any further questions please contact us, we are pleased to help.

My order exceeded £10.00 in value, where is my item?
Most of our orders that exceed £10.00 in value are sent recorded delivery. If there is no tracking information on your order please contact us for further assistance. Any items sent by recorded post can be tracked via the Royal Mail website by entering the tracking number into the Track & Trace facility.

My order was despatched by courier, where is my item?
All courier deliveries are tracked and insured. If there is no tracking information on your order please contact us for further assistance.

2. Combined postage

Do you offer combined postage discounts?
Yes, many of our items are eligible for reduced P&P on combined purchases. Some items when combined with others are posted free of charge. Please browse our store to take full advantage of the offers available. Please contact us if you require further assistance.

3. Payment option

What payment methods do you accept?
We only accept PayPal: it is the safest and easiest way to pay on eBay. We do not accept any other payment methods.

 Tip
A little time spent setting up your FAQs will save hours answering the same questions over and over again.

Step 25 above:
returns policy/terms and conditions

Returns policy:
You may cancel your order any time within seven (7) days, beginning on the day that you received the goods. We will refund the price of the goods in full; however the delivery costs originally paid are non-refundable unless your entire order is cancelled within seven (7) days of receipt of goods. You must notify us in writing via the eBay messaging system of your intent to return within seven (7) days of receipt of the item. You will be responsible for the cost of returning the goods to us. If a refund is payable to you we will process the refund as soon as possible, and, in any case within thirty (30) days of the day you gave written notice of cancellation. 'Get It Fast' purchases sent by Royal Mail Special Delivery are non-refundable, defective goods will be replaced only. If the defective

item is out of stock, the customer will be issued a credit note that can be used to purchase other items from us. The credit will not include the P&P charges, but any purchase made using the credit note will be posted Free of Charge by our economy postal service. To cancel an order you must return the goods to us immediately. The goods must be returned in the same condition in which you received them, and they will be returned at your own cost and risk. You have a legal obligation to take reasonable care of the goods while they are in your possession. If you fail to comply with this obligation, we may have a right of action against you for compensation. This applies to all goods that are returned. Our returns policy does not affect your statutory rights. If you return goods claiming they are defective, we will examine the returned goods and will notify you of your refund via email within a reasonable period of time. We will process the refund due to you as soon as possible and, in any case within thirty (30) days of the day we confirm via email that you are entitled to a refund for defective goods. Any orders for personalised goods are non-returnable. Please note that this does not affect your statutory rights. If a refund is payable to you, the refund will be issued to your PayPal account. Please return your goods to: ***INSERT ADDRESS HERE***. If you have a query about returning goods, please contact our Customer Services team through the eBay messaging system.

Terms and conditions:
Any communications should be conducted through the eBay messaging system. We will not be held responsible for any loss or inconvenience when communications are sent by any other means. All messages sent through the eBay messaging system will receive a response within 24 hrs. By clicking the 'Buy It Now' button you agree to adhere to our terms and conditions of sale and our returns policy. Postage and Packaging prices (including discounts and promotional capped rates) quoted are applicable to most areas of the Mainland UK; some areas (most notably but not limited to Northern Ireland, Scottish Highlands and Channel Islands) may be subject to further charges. The promotional capped rate postage charge is limited to

a combined weight not exceeding 15 kg. If a combined purchase exceeds 2 kg in weight it will be despatched by courier regardless of whichever postal service is selected by the buyer.

OPENING AN eBAY SHOP

http://pages.ebay.co.uk/storefronts/start.html

In order to open an eBay shop a seller needs to meet certain requirements:

Basic Shop – You must have a minimum feedback score of 10 or you must be PayPal verified

Featured or Anchor Shop – You must be a registered business seller on eBay, you must be PayPal verified and you must maintain a twelve-month average Detailed Seller Ratings score of 4.4 or above in each of the four categories

ADVANTAGES

There are several advantages to operating an eBay shop:

1. It says to potential buyers 'I am seriously committed to my eBay business'
2. Your listing fees are halved. If you are listing upwards of 150 items the basic shop will pay for itself in listing fee discounts alone. If you are listing more than 300 items it is worthwhile upgrading to a featured shop as you are eligible for further discounts
3. You can effectively pause your listings by applying holiday settings to your shop and set up out-of-office auto-responses on the eBay messaging system

If you intend to run more than 300 listings per month a 'featured shop' is a worthwhile investment as your listing fees are halved again, so the extra outlay is recouped in discounts alone. You also receive further search-result ranking boosts and access to more detailed report software.

SHOP DESIGN

The eBay shops are user customisable and you can change the design of the shop very quickly and easily to suit your requirements. There are several preset templates and colour schemes to choose from that will give your shop the professional look you want to achieve.

Further down the road it would be wise to invest in employing the services of a web designer to take full advantage of all of the design features available to endow your store and listings with a professional finish. There are many eBay shop and listing design specialists advertising on the internet. Prices vary widely so be sure to shop around for the best deal. Try http://www. kookiweb.co.uk as a starting point.

👍**Tip**

Try to make the colours of your shop reflect your brand – a theme running throughout will achieve a professional look.

SETTING UP YOUR eBAY SHOP

As a start-up, we would recommend selecting the basic shop to begin with; you can always upgrade at a later date if required. Follow the steps below:

1. Log into your eBay account
2. Type the following URL into your browser: http://pages.
    ebay.co.uk/storefronts/start.html
3. There is some advice regarding opening an eBay shop and
    within the text is a link to 'open an eBay shop'. Click the link
4. Select which level of subscription you require
5. Name your shop
6. Click the 'Continue' button
7. Select to add the Selling Manager Pro and Reports packages
    to your subscription; they are free
8. Check the box to accept the user agreement
9. Click 'Subscribe'

MANAGING YOUR eBAY SHOP

Now you have a shop and have subscribed to Selling Manager
Pro, at the bottom right corner of your Summary page is a
'Manage My Shop' window. Various tasks can be completed
from this location.

We have already mentioned the holiday settings, and these are
dealt with in more detail in the 'Using Holiday Settings' section
of Chapter 5. For now we'll concentrate on the display settings
and shop categories.

Display settings

These settings will affect the way your shop looks. You will be
able to select a theme, and change the colours and fonts used in
that theme. The options and possibilities are endless.

Shop categories

These settings will decide how your buyer navigates around
your shop. Similar to eBay's categories it will allow your

customers to navigate quickly to the items of interest within your shop. For example, if you have a jewellery shop, you may want a category each for rings, earrings, necklaces, bracelets and watches, then subcategories within your 'rings' category for engagement, wedding, signet, eternity and so on. You can also break down these subcategories into further sub-subcategories.

For example: Your 'engagement' subcategory could have subcategories for 9-carat Gold, 24-carat Gold and Platinum.

Changing the display settings

Follow the steps below:

1. Navigate to the 'Manage My Shop' window at the bottom right corner of your Summary page
2. Click the 'Display Settings' link
3. Beside the heading 'Basic Information' click 'Change'
4. Update your shop description
5. Select a predefined logo or, if you have designed a logo, upload your own
6. Click 'Save Settings'
7. Scroll down the page to 'Theme & Display'
8. Click 'Change to another theme'
9. Select a theme that most closely suits your needs. There is a choice of Left Navigation, Top Navigation and Easily Customisable. The most popular shop themes can also be viewed
10. Click the 'Save Settings' button
11. Click 'Edit current theme' to change the colours and fonts displayed on your shop front if required
12. Click the 'Save Settings' button

Leave the other settings at the default eBay settings for now. They are customisable but will perform their function for the time being and can be adjusted to suit your specific requirements at a later date if you choose.

Adding shop categories

Follow the steps below:

1. Navigate to the 'Manage My Shop' window at the bottom right corner of your Summary page
2. Click the 'Display Settings' link
3. Click the 'Shop Categories' link in the navigation bar at the left hand side of the page
4. Click the 'add category' button
5. Enter into the fields the names of the categories you wish to add to your shop
6. Click the 'Save' button
7. To create a subcategory, click on the category you would like to add the subcategory to
8. Click the 'Add Category' button.
9. Enter into the fields the names of the subcategories you wish to add
10. Click the 'Save' button
11. To create a sub-subcategory, click on the subcategory you would like to add a sub-subcategory to
12. Click on the 'add category' button

This is the final layer available to you: no further subcategories can be added to your sub-subcategories.

The basic settings for your shop have now been completed. There are other functions available for more advanced users;

help and assistance regarding these functions is available from the eBay help pages.

 Tip
Use your shop categories effectively – it will make it easier for buyers to browse your store and they will buy more.

USING SELLING MANAGER PRO

http://pages.ebay.co.uk/selling_manager_pro

Selling Manager Pro provides you with useful tools that will automate many of the time-consuming tasks involved in running an eBay business, such as leaving feedback and communicating with your buyers. This useful add-on will also provide you with invoices, address labels and packing-slip templates, so it really is a must-have option.

SUBSCRIBING TO SELLING MANAGER PRO

If you have already signed up for an eBay shop you will have received this package free of charge as part of the subscription.

If not, complete the following steps:

1. Type the following into your browser: http://pages.ebay. co.uk/selling_manager_pro
2. Click the 'Subscribe now' button

Now that you have subscribed to Selling Manager Pro (SMP) the default page that 'My eBay' opens on will be your SMP Summary. This page provides lots of information about the current state of your business and also provides many useful links and tools. Set this webpage as your browser's homepage: you will be using this page often.

SETTING UP SMP

The only thing you need to set up are your automation preferences:

1. From the SMP Summary page click the 'Automation preferences' link in the navigation bar on the left-hand side of the page
2. Check the box to 'Automatically leave the Following Positive feedback'
3. Select the option 'Buyer has paid for this item and left me positive Feedback'
4. Click the link to 'Edit stored comments' if you wish to customise eBay's default selection of five comments that will be chosen at random

The basic options for SMP are now set up. There are numerous other features that you can explore at your leisure with detailed assistance available in the eBay help pages should you have any difficulty.

👍 **Tip**

Automating your feedback will save you lots of time and keep your buyers happy.

USING TURBO LISTER

http://pages.ebay.co.uk/turbo_lister

This free download for listing your items is far simpler, better and faster than the eBay listing tool.

DOWNLOADING TURBO LISTER

1. Type the following address into your browser: http://pages. ebay.co.uk/turbo_lister
2. Click the 'Download Now' button
3. Select 'Run'

Once the application is downloaded, launch the programme and we will guide you through the set-up process.

INITIAL SET UP

Complete the following steps:

1. Hover the mouse over 'File', then 'New' and click 'User File' at the bottom of the dropdown menu
2. Select to 'Create a new Turbo Lister file'
3. Click 'Next'
4. Enter your eBay username
5. Click the 'Next' button
6. Click the 'Connect now' button
7. Click the 'Continue' button
8. Sign in to your eBay account
9. Click 'I Agree'
10. Check your contact information
11. Click the 'Next' button
12. Select 'Synchronise your data with eBay'
13. Click the 'Finish' button
14. Close the popup window
15. Click the 'Synchronise Now' button

IMPORTING YOUR SHOP CATEGORIES

Complete the following steps:

1.   Click on 'Tools'
2.   Click on 'Program Updates' from the dropdown menu
3.   Click the 'Install Now' button

TURBO LISTER OPTIONS SET UP

All of the navigation for this set up is completed via the navigation bar on the left-hand side of the options window:

1.   Click 'Tools', then 'Options'
2.   In the navigation bar to the left-hand side of the options window click 'Personal Information', then 'eBay Account'
3.   Check your eBay user ID is correct
4.   Click 'PayPal Account' in the navigation bar
5.   Check that your PayPal account details are correct.
6.   Click 'Seller Options' in the navigation bar
7.   Click 'eBay Sites'
8.   Check the box beside 'eBay United Kingdom'
9.   Click 'Default Site & Format' in the navigation bar
10.   Select 'eBay United Kingdom' from the dropdown menu
11.   Check the box next to 'Fixed Price'
12.   Click 'Fixed Price Defaults' in the navigation bar
13.   Click 'eBay United Kingdom'
14.   Click 'Listing Upgrades'. If you are intending to list most of your items in the Home and Garden, or Clothes Shoes and Accessories categories these upgrades are free, so select to add them as a default
15.   Click 'Payment Methods'
16.   Check the box beside PayPal
17.   Check the boxes beside any other payment methods you are happy to accept
18.   Click 'Additional Instructions'

19. Type into the field your terms and conditions of sale (for an example, see 'eBay customisable texts' in the 'Opening a Seller's Account on eBay' section earlier in this chapter)
20. Click 'Returns Policy & Warranty'
21. Type into the field your returns policy
22. Click 'Buyer Requirements'
23. Set the options up as you did in the eBay set-up process
24. Click 'Advanced options'
25. Check the boxes to 'Automatically download updates' and 'Automatically back up user database'
26. Click the 'Apply' button
27. Click the 'Okay' button

All options selected here will appear on all listings of that type, so only include information that you want to appear on every listing you compile.

FOLDERS

While you have Turbo Lister open it is a good idea to create folders in your inventory that directly relate to your shop categories. This will make it easier for you to locate your listings should you require them at a later date. It is a very simple task:

1. Locate the 'Inventory' window in the top left corner of the Turbo Lister main screen
2. Right-click on the 'My Items' folder
3. Click 'New Folder'
4. Repeat this process as many times as you want to create any number of folders in which to store your listings
5. Create subfolders by right-clicking on your new folders
6. Create sub-subfolders by right-clicking on your subfolders

Organising your folders in this way creates a system similar to your eBay shop and will make navigating either your Turbo Lister files or your shop a breeze.

MAINTENANCE

Maintenance of your Turbo Lister is a simple affair: you need to check for updates and synchronise with your eBay account. Complete these steps when you launch the program for the first time each day:

1. Click on the 'Tools' button in the taskbar
2. Click on 'Check for program updates'
3. Download any updates required
4. Click on the 'Synchronise' button
5. Click the 'Synchronise Now' button in the pop-up window

 Tip

Turbo Lister's 'Good 'Til Cancelled' rule will automatically relist your items until they have all sold.

USING PHOTOBUCKET

www.photobucket.com

Photobucket, a secure online photo-hosting website, can be used to enhance your photos and insert them into your item listing description.

OPENING AN ACCOUNT

1. Type the URL into your web browser: www.photobucket.com

2. Click the 'Sign up' link
3. Complete the form
4. Click the 'Sign me up' button

ORGANISING YOUR PHOTOBUCKET

In order to make your Photobucket easy to use, I would recommend organising a file system similar to your Turbo Lister system and eBay shop category system. You will be surprised how often you will want access to your photos.

Operating a system like this to store your photos will make life much simpler for you when it comes to locating them for future use:

1. Sign into your Photobucket account
2. Roll your mouse over the 'Album' button on the main Photobucket navigation bar
3. Click the 'Organise' button in the dropdown menu
4. In the navigation bar on the left-hand side of the page click the 'Create Album' button
5. Title your album and check the box to make the album private (unless you wish to share your photos with the world), and remember to make all of your albums private every time you create a new one
6. Once again click the 'Create Album' link and create your next album, continuing the process until you have an album for each of your product categories
7. If you want to make sub-albums within your new albums in order to continue matching the system to your other file systems in Turbo Lister or your eBay shop, click the 'Create Album' button
8. Title your album as before

9. Check the box to 'Add as an album to'
10. Select the album in which you want to create your sub-album from the dropdown menu
11. Click the 'Add album' button
12. Continue to repeat this process creating albums and sub-albums to match each of your Turbo Lister or eBay shop folders

There is nothing else you need to know about Photobucket until it comes to listing your item for sale (see Chapter 4), but there are many features available to you that you may want to employ later such as photo-editing tools and folder themes.

👍**Tip**

To keep your costs low, upload your photos to Photobucket for free within the main body of your listing on the types of listings where eBay charges for more than one photo.

USING AUCTIVA

www.Auctiva.com

Auctiva is a free online eBay management tool primarily used by eBay sellers for cross-promotional purposes. You can use it to promote your other items on each of your listings.

ACCOUNT SET-UP

1. Type the URL into your web browser: www.Auctiva.com
2. Enter your intended username, password and email address
3. Click the box to agree to the terms and conditions

4. Click to 'Start your free trial'
5. Click the button to 'Generate Token'
6. Enter your eBay username and password
7. Click 'I agree' to allow Auctiva access to your account
8. Roll your mouse over the 'My Account' button on the main navigation bar
9. Click on the 'Pick a Plan' button
10. Choose the 'Free' plan

SETTING UP YOUR CROSS-PROMOTIONAL TOOL

Follow the steps below:

1. Roll your mouse over the 'Stores' button on the main Auctiva navigation bar and click on the scrolling gallery
2. Choose 'Style' and select the layout and type of gallery you require
3. Choose 'Colours' and select the palette to match your eBay shop; there are some preset options to choose from or you can specify your choices by either entering the Hex HTML code or by selecting the colour by clicking on the small box beneath each heading and using the colour-picker tool
4. Text and placement: customise the text contained within your gallery and specify where the gallery is placed within your listing
5. Display options: select the option most suited to your needs; this will probably be the 'Random Selection' option. You can also specify if there are items that you want to include in or exclude from every gallery
6. When you have finished setting up your gallery click 'Save'

The gallery will now appear automatically in every listing you upload to eBay.

👍 **Tip**

Cross-promoting your items is free advertising for your other products – use the Auctiva tools and listing description to best effect.

SETTING UP A ROYAL MAIL ONLINE BUSINESS ACCOUNT

https://www.royalmail.com/discounts-payment/credit-account/online-business-account

For an eBay trader, setting up an account with the Royal Mail is essential; their delivery options are second to none. The advantages from which an account holder benefits are numerous, and the Royal Mail will tailor the service to your requirements.

Visit the above web address or phone the Royal Mail on 08457 959950 for information regarding your specific requirements and the application process.

Services to consider as an eBay trader sending regular amounts of large letters and packets are:

PACKETPOST

If you are sending more than 5,000 items per year, Packetpost will offer large savings over regular tariffs. Charges are based on the average weight and format of all the items you are sending with the Royal Mail on a particular day. The formats available include 1st and 2nd Class Letters, Large Letters, Packets, Recorded Deliveries, Special Deliveries, International Signed For and Airsure. The maximum weight available to send by 2nd Class Post increases from 1 kg to 2 kg, and there is a choice of daily or fixed rate charging options.

PACKETSORT

If you are sending more than 250 items per day the Packetsort option becomes available to you. It is similar to Packetpost, but by sorting the post into eight postcode groups before handing it over you are rewarded with further discounts on the Packetpost tariff.

COLLECTIONS SERVICE

For a relatively small annual fee (currently £775 plus VAT, which works out to just over £17 per week) the Royal Mail will collect from you on a regular daily basis. This option is well worth considering; when you weigh up the cost of running a vehicle and the time it will save you travelling to and from the mail centre or sorting office, it really does seem like quite a bargain.

PRINTED POSTAGE IMPRESSION

When you sign up for an online business account you will be provided with a link from which to download your Printed Postage Impression (PPI). This is the image that appears on prepaid post and will be unique to your account.

Download the 22 x 80 mm images for first- and second-class post and keep them in a file on your desktop called 'PPIs'.

PPI TEMPLATES

Now create four Word documents with the following titles (FP stands for full page, i.e. a page full of repeated PPIs):

1st Class PPI
2nd Class PPI
1st Class FP
2nd Class FP

These documents will allow you to add your PPI to your despatch labels or print a sheet of PPIs for use on correspondence and so on.

1. Open the document '1st Class PPI'
2. Click the 'File' button, then 'Page Setup'
3. Set the margins: top 1.1 cm; right 2 cm
4. Click the 'Insert' button, roll your mouse over 'Picture' and select 'From file'
5. Locate the 'PPIs' folder on the desktop and select the 1st Class PPI
6. Click the 'Format' button, and click 'Paragraph ...'
7. In the 'Indents and Spacing' tab, under the 'General' heading, select Alignment: 'Right' from the dropdown menu
8. Save the document

Repeat this process for the 2nd Class PPI document.
Now open the document '1st Class FP'.

1. Click the 'File' button, then 'Page Setup'. Set the margins to 1.5 cm all round
2. Click the 'Insert' button, roll your mouse over 'Picture' and select 'From file'
3. Locate the 'PPIs' folder on the desktop and select the 1st Class PPI
4. Right-click the image and select 'Copy'
5. Right-click on the page and select 'Paste'
6. Repeat this process until the page is full of 1st Class PPIs
7. Space them out evenly to make it easier for you to cut them out when required

Repeat this process for the 2nd Class FP document.

Now that you have these files stored on your computer it is simply a matter of running your invoices/packing slips back through the printer to add your PPI to them. This process is dealt with in more depth in the 'Printing Your Despatch Notes' section of Chapter 5.

REGISTERING WITH PARCEL2GO

www.parcel2go.com

Parcel2Go provide cheap and reliable courier services from a range of companies. All shipments will be insured and tracked, and a proof of delivery will be obtained.

ACCOUNT REGISTRATION

Follow the steps below:

1. Type the URL into your web browser: www.parcel2go.com
2. Click on the 'Login/Register' link in the top left corner of the web page
3. Click on the 'Register' link
4. Complete the short form
5. Click on the 'Create User' button
6. Click the 'Return Home' button

ACCOUNT SET-UP

Follow the steps below:

1. Click the 'Login' button under the heading 'My Account' on the right-hand side of the page
2. Click on the 'My Details' tab
3. Scroll down to 'Addresses'

4. Click 'Click here to add an address'
5. Click the 'UK' button
6. Enter your postcode and click the 'Find Address' button
7. Select your address from the dropdown menu
8. Click the 'Use Address' button
9. Complete the details on the remainder of the form
10. Click the checkbox to make it the default address
11. Click the 'Integration' tab
12. Click the 'click here' link next to 'Want to get started' under the 'eBay Item Shipping' heading
13. Enter your eBay user ID
14. Click the 'Submit' button
15. Sign in to your eBay account
16. Click the 'I Agree' button to grant account access to Parcel2Go

Now when it comes to despatching your parcels that are too large or not cost effective to send with the Royal Mail, you can download your addresses and despatch details to Parcel2Go: this makes the process extremely fast and simple.

 Tip
Send your higher value items by one of the tracked, recorded or courier services – one loss can seriously damage your profit.

4
CREATING YOUR LISTING

ANATOMY OF A LISTING

Your listing needs to take all the information related to the item you are selling and transmit it to your buyer in an interesting, concise and straightforward manner. All of the elements included in a listing are included below with a brief description. More in-depth advice relating to each element is included later in this chapter.

TITLE AND SUBTITLE

Your title is singularly the most important part of your listing. It is more important than your description, photo and price. However, these too play an integral part in encouraging the sales.

Please refer to the 'Choosing the Right Title and Subtitle' section later in this chapter for more information.

PHOTOGRAPH

The second most important aspect that will drive people to your listing over your competitors is your photograph.

Please refer to the 'Photographing Your Items' section later in this chapter for more information.

DESCRIPTION

This is your chance to provide the fine details and convince your buyer to place their purchase with you.

Please refer to the Writing Your Listing Description section later in this chapter for more information.

CHOOSING THE RIGHT TITLE AND SUBTITLE

The title is the most important aspect of your listing because, without it, your buyers will have great difficulty finding your item. Having the right title can make or break your sales figures; miss out an important keyword and you will miss out on sales; choose the correct keyword and your sales figures can soar.

TITLE

The eBay search engine works in a similar way to all other search engines. It uses the keywords of the item title to satisfy the customer's search query and locate the product for which they are searching.

The best way to approach this task is to ask yourself: 'What would I enter into the search bar if I was looking for this item?' If you have someone else to hand, ask them what they would enter if they were looking for the item. You'll be surprised by what you hear. Then compare your results with other sellers to see what they have included in their title that is driving people to their listing. Very often you will find that one keyword in particular is extremely effective and if your title is missing this keyword you will miss out on sales.

Ensure you have included in your title any specifics that your buyer may search for, for example: colours, materials, brands, sizes, dimensions and quantity.

Try not to waste words with 'and' 'or' 'l@@k' etc. It is a waste of your precious characters.

There are several widely used abbreviations or words used by eBay sellers to get a message across to the buyer without using too many characters, for example:

BN – Brand New
BNIB – Brand New In Box/Bag
BNIP – Brand New In Packaging
BNWT – Brand New With Tags
VGC – Very Good Condition
Mint – Like New

Your title needs to make sense rather than being a jumble of keywords. Play with the order of the words and read it back to yourself until it makes sense.

For example, if you are selling a Magimix Kettle model number 11695 your title should look something like this:

Magimix Kettle Polished Stainless Steel Chrome Black 1.8L 240V 3000w 11695 BNIB.

 Tip

Use every character available in your eBay title – don't waste characters with words such as: 'and', 'with', 'L@@K', 'or' and so on.

103

SUBTITLE

eBay charges a significant amount to provide a subtitle on your listing, which prevents many sellers from utilising this service, but this is a very good means of making your listing stand out from others at the gallery stage.

The subtitle is the perfect place to entice buyers to purchase from you by informing them of your service, for example: 'Same Day Despatch, Next Day Delivery & 1 Year Manufacturer's Warranty' or '24hr Despatch & Huge Discounts Available for Multiple Purchases'.

Due to the expense you will need to decide if it is worth adding a subtitle to your listing as the charge for adding one will be incurred every time the item relists. As a rule it is generally worthwhile to add a subtitle to your listing when you need to communicate a special service to your buyer at the gallery stage to set your listing apart from the competition. If you do not have any competition don't use a subtitle: it will eat into your profit margin.

PHOTOGRAPHING YOUR ITEMS

The photographs you use on your listing are second only in importance to your title: the saying that people 'buy with their eyes' is true. You need to present your item in the best possible way that you can.

Stock photos are available for many items. Locating a stock photo for your item will save you lots of time and you will be rewarded with a professional-looking image for your listing. Try the manufacturer's website, your supplier's website or Google/ Bing images before taking the photos yourself. Please ensure that you are not infringing copyright laws by using the images.

If you need or prefer to take your own images, try to photograph several items at the same time. You will save time by negating the need to keep setting up your photo area, camera and so on.

CAMERA

Good-quality digital cameras are relatively cheap to acquire, but you need to ensure that the camera has all of the options required to achieve a quality listing photograph.

The camera must have zoom and macro functions for getting in close to the subject and photographing fine details and defects; a large memory or an ability to expand the memory by using memory cards and a rechargeable battery or mains power source. You don't want to be scrabbling around for more batteries when trying to upload your photos.

LOCATION

In order to achieve a professional-looking image for your item listings choose a readily available location that is suitable to display your items in their best light. Ensure that the area is clean and free from background objects that could distract the eye. For example, kitchen items could be photographed on a particular section of your kitchen worktop. Try to keep the location of your photographs consistent between listings: this portrays a professional look when your buyer views your shop or browses your listings.

COMPILING THE PHOTOGRAPH

Take the item out of the packaging and take a little time to arrange it in a pleasing way. For best results use natural light, a flash will distort colours and add unwanted highlights. Try to make your item fill the frame and take several photographs from different angles; also photograph any small details that could interest the buyer. If the item you are selling has variations (i.e. available in five different colours) photograph all of the items together (for your main listing photo) and individually (for each variation).

☝ **Tip**

Use stock images if available – you will save bundles of time and get a professional photo for free. Just make sure you avoid watermarked and copyrighted images.

If your item is reflective try to take the photo from an angle that will not show unwanted reflections. It looks very unprofessional to have yourself captured taking the photo in the reflection on your item.

PHOTO EDITING

Upload your photos to your computer. Rotate your images so that they are all oriented in the correct manner. Most computers or cameras are supplied with photo-editing software that will give you the ability to improve your photos. Many have an auto-fix option that will enhance colours and sharpen images: use it. Crop your photos to remove unwanted areas, ensure that the item is the focus of the image and ensure that the item fills the photograph. If this is done at the photography stage it saves you time at the photo-editing stage.

View your images and select the best photo to use as your main listing image. Select a few other images to use in your listing and delete any unwanted images: they will only take up space on your computer and confuse you when it comes to listing the item.

Do not resize your main listing photos: the larger the image the better. Many of eBay listing types feature free supersize photos and this allows your buyer to view the product close up and in great detail.

Resize the photos that you would like to appear in your item description to the size that you would like them to appear on the listing. Ensure that all of the photos appearing in your item description are of a similar size (approx 400 x 500 pixels is a good, manageable size). Resizing your photos now will save time when it comes to uploading your photos to a hosting site and when compiling your listing.

PHOTO HOSTING

Store your photos on your computer or a separate hard drive or both. We would recommend archiving your photos in a file system similar to the ones we set up in Photobucket or Turbo Lister earlier in the guide, but while they are in use keep them easily to hand in a folder on your desktop titled 'eBay items to list' or something similar.

There are several photo-hosting websites available but for ease of use we recommend Photobucket, and you should have registered an account already (see 'Using Photobucket' in Chapter 3).

👍 Tip

Take items out of the packaging and display them effectively on a corresponding background before photographing them.

WRITING YOUR LISTING DESCRIPTION

A listing description should provide your buyer with all the information they are likely to require before purchasing your item. If you do not include all of the relevant information in your listing you are likely to either drive buyers to another listing that provides the information they are looking for, or be inundated with questions from buyers seeking further information.

SOURCES OF INFORMATION

There are several sources from which you can obtain the information required to complete your listing:

Packaging

Check the packaging of your item: it will often include a description and or details specific to the item such as weight, dimensions or product specifications.

Manufacturer

Check the manufacturer's website: you can sometimes source all of the information required for your listing.

eBay

If your item is already selling on eBay this is a great place to start. You must never use another seller's description or photograph, but you can use it for research.

👍 **Tip**

Keep your description clear and to the point: a small paragraph describing item uses and specifics, a bullet-point list of features and a short explanation of services offered are all that are required.

Internet

A search for the product on the internet will often provide you with a great wealth of information.

COMMUNICATING INFORMATION TO YOUR BUYER

Once you have sourced the information, you need to communicate it to your buyer in a concise easy-to-read factual manner. For example:

<u>Large Traditional Umbrella Cupcake Design</u>
This fantastic umbrella is traditionally styled with a strong wooden centre pole and curved handle. The canopy features an attractive cupcake pattern on a pastel blue background. The umbrella measures 89 cm (35 in) in length and has a generous diameter of 102 cm (40 in) when open.

Features:
- Strong 8-spoke design
- Traditional styling
- Safety spoke ends
- Velcro securing strap
- 102 cm (40 in) diameter canopy
- 89 cm (35 in) overall length

PHOTOS

You can insert photos into your description using Photobucket's image-hosting service. Where you choose to insert them is a matter of personal preference.

It is a worthwhile exercise to include extra photos in your description rather than adding them to your listing as they do not incur fees and can provide your buyer with more information. Use close-up photographs of fine details or points of interest that may entice your buyer into completing their purchase.

STARTING YOUR OWN eBAY BUSINESS

OTHER IMPORTANT INFORMATION

You should also use the item description to communicate to your buyers why they should buy from you rather than the competition. Tell them about your despatch options and discounts, alternative related items or complementary items that you also sell. Encourage your buyers to view your shop or other listings: when buyers make multiple purchases you save money in despatch costs and PayPal fees. For example:

All of our items are in stock and ready for dispatch

Any purchases made before 2 p.m. (Mon–Fri) will be despatched SAME DAY

Any purchases made after 2 p.m. are despatched NEXT WORKING DAY

Please browse our items – we offer MASSIVE discounts on multiple purchases

CREATING THE LISTING TEMPLATES

Now let's set up some templates for your listings. You may want different templates according to the type of product you are selling or for different brands; anything is possible and you can store as many templates as you want.

We found it easiest to have different templates for the different despatch types. For example: Letters, Large Letters, Packages, Courier Items.

SETTING UP A NEW TEMPLATE

Follow the steps below:

1. Launch Turbo Lister
2. Click 'New', then 'Create New Template'

A pop-up window will appear; this is where you will compile your 'Large Letter' template.

Most of the fields will need to be customised for each separate listing, but if there is anything that is applicable to all of the listings that you intend to compile using this template, enter the information into the relevant field.

👍**Tip**

Take the time to create a selection of templates – they will save you stacks of time in the long run.

TITLE AND CATEGORY SECTION

Title

Use the Title field to name your template to suit your requirements, for example 'Small Package Template 01' if you are selling a large amount of items that will be posted as a small package, or 'Kitchen Small Appliances 01' if you are selling a wide range of similar items in the same category.

Subtitle

If you intend to use a subtitle on every listing that states 'Next day delivery available on this item' or 'Massive discounts available for purchases of more than 10' enter it into the template.

Category

Complete the 'Category' field if you are selling many items in the same category; if you are not, ensure you leave this field blank because any listings created using this template will default to the chosen category and mistakes may happen. To choose the correct category for your item:

1. Click on the 'Select' button
2. Select the 'search categories' tab in the new pop-up window
3. Enter a brief description or the name of your item into the search field and you will be rewarded with a selection of categories that are suitable to host the listing of your item
4. Choose the most appropriate result for your item
5. This will open an 'Item Specifics' window. Once again, leave these blank if the specifics of the items you are listing in this category vary, or complete them if the specifics relate to all the items you will be listing using this template

Once you have completed the 'Category' field you will be allowed the option of adding a second category. This is useful if, for example, you are selling unisex umbrellas: eBay does not have a category for unisex items, so you would need to sell your items in both Men's Accessories/Umbrellas and Women's Accessories/Umbrellas.

Shop categories

If you have an eBay shop you can specify which of your shop categories should feature the items your template is designed around by selecting the appropriate category from the two dropdown menus provided.

UPC/EAN/ISBN/VIN

The UPC/EAN/ISBN/VIN field is provided so that you can provide your customers with the barcode information for the product you are offering for sale. This field should not be completed at this stage as the information will vary from item to item.

PICTURES AND DESCRIPTION SECTION

Pictures

It is very unlikely that you will be able to use one photo for all of the items that you will be listing using this template so leave the photograph fields blank and proceed directly to the description: this is where most of your time and effort will be spent, and this section should be completed with particular attention to detail and thought.

👍 **Tip**

Ensure that you have included all necessary details in your Title, e.g. colour, size, measurement, brand and condition.

Description

Turbo Lister provides a 'Description Builder'. This is very similar to the eBay listing builder and will convert your built listing into HTML code automatically. The description field will show the code when you have finished using the builder. Any further code-editing you wish to carry out can be done in this field without the need to reopen the builder:

1. Select the 'HTML View' tab
2. If you have created a shop or company logo and uploaded it to Photobucket, open Photobucket in another tab on your browser
3. Locate your logo image on Photobucket
4. Roll your mouse over the image
5. Left-click the section of code marked 'HTML Code' (this will copy the code)

6. Paste the code into the Turbo Lister description window. You should see something like this:

```
<a   href='http://s1083.photobucket.com/albums/j391/
ebaybus/Logo/?action=view&amp;current=ebuslogo.png'
target='_blank'><img  src='http://i1083.Photobucket.com/
albums/j391/  ebaybus/Logo/ebuslogo.png'  border='0'
alt='Photobucket'></a>
```

7. Type this code in front of the pasted code: <P align=center> and this code at the end: </P>

8. You should see something like this:

```
<P align=center><a  href='http://s1083.photobucket.com/
albums/j391/ebaybus/Logo/?action=view&amp;current=ebu
slogo.png' target='_blank'><img src='http://i1083.Photobucket.
com/albums/j391/ebaybus/Logo/ebuslogo.png'  border='0'
alt='Photobucket'></a></P>
```

Your logo will now appear centralised at the top of the template description and in exactly the same place on any listing you compile in the future using this template

9. Next, you need to add the Item Title

10. Type the following:

```
<P align=center><STRONG><U><FONT size=6 face=Arial>***
REPLACE WITH ITEM TITLE***</FONT></U></STRONG></P>
```

Now whenever you need to create a listing it is simply a matter of replacing the asterixed text by typing the Item Title in its place

11. The next step is to add the description itself

12. Type the following:

```
<P align=left><FONT size=5 face=Arial>***REPLACE WITH
ITEM DESCRIPTION TEXT***</FONT></P>
```

Adding the description is now a matter of replacing the asterixed text with the text of your choice

13. Now we can add the bullet points to provide our buyers with a list of the features relevant to the item

14. Type the following:

```
<P align=left><FONT size=5 face=Arial><STRONG><U>
Features:</U></STRONG></FONT></P>
<UL>
<LI>
<DIV align=left><FONT size=5 face=Arial>
***REPLACE WITH TEXT FOR BULLET POINT 1***
</FONT></DIV>
<LI>
<DIV align=left><FONT size=5 face=Arial>
***REPLACE WITH TEXT FOR BULLET POINT 2***
</FONT></DIV>
<LI>
<DIV align=left><FONT size=5 face=Arial>
***REPLACE WITH TEXT FOR BULLET POINT 3***
</FONT></DIV>
<LI>
<DIV align=left><FONT size=5 face=Arial>
***REPLACE WITH TEXT FOR BULLET POINT 4***
</FONT></DIV></LI></UL>
```

As before you can now simply insert the text you require. It is a simple process to add in extra bullet points if the need arises. It is recommended that you set your template up with four or five bullet points, then add or reduce this number if you find that you do not regularly use them all or regularly require more

15 Next, we need to add a section for our extra photographs:

```
<P align=center>***REPLACE WITH LINKS TO PHOTOBUCKET
***</P>
```

Adding photos into your description is now simply a matter of replacing the asterixed code with the code supplied by Photobucket. All you will need to do is:

i.   Roll your mouse over the photo of your choice

ii. Click on the code marked 'HTML Code'

iii. Paste the code in place of the '★★★REPLACE WITH LINKS TO PHOTOBUCKET★★★' text in the Turbo Lister HTML editor

iv. If you have more than one photo repeat this process for each photo you want to insert. Ensure that you allow a space between the pieces of pasted code to allow the photos to distribute themselves appropriately in the listing. For example:

```
<P align=center><A href='http://s1083.photobucket.com/
albums/j391/ebaybus/?action=view&amp;current=photo1.
jpg' target=_blank><IMG border=0 alt=Photobucket
src='http://i1083.photobucket.com/albums/j391/
ebaybus/photo1.jpg'></A> <A href='http://s1083.
photobucket.com/albums/j391/ebabybus/?action=view&a
mp;current=photo2.jpg' target=_blank><IMG border=0
alt=Photobucket src='http://i1083.photobucket.com/
albums/j391/ebaybus/photo2.jpg'></A> <A href='http://
s1083.photobucket.com/albums/j391/ebaybus/?action=vi
ew&amp;current=photo3.jpg' target=_blank><IMG border=0
alt=Photobucket src='http://i1083.photobucket.com/
albums/j391/ebaybus/photo3.jpg'></A> <A href='http://
s1083.photobucket.com/albums/j391/ebaybus/?action=vi
ew&amp;current=photo4.jpg' target=_blank><IMG border=0
alt=Photobucket src='http://i1083.photobucket.com/
albums/j391/ebaybus/photo4.jpg'></A></P>
```

Tip
Use the listing designer's themes with your seasonal listings
for maximum effect during holiday periods.

16. Now we need to communicate any other information we
    may want to provide to our buyer, change the text to suit
    your requirements:

```
<P align=center><FONT size=6 face=Arial><STRONG><U>
All of our items are in stock and ready for despatch
</U></STRONG></FONT></P>
<P align=center><FONT size=6 face=Arial><STRONG><U>
Any purchases made before 2 p.m. (Mon–Fri) will be despatched
SAME DAY
</U></STRONG></FONT></P>
<P align=center><FONT size=6 face=Arial><STRONG><U>
Any purchases made after 2 p.m. are despatched NEXT WORKING
DAY
</U></STRONG></FONT></P>
<P align=center><FONT size=6 face=Arial><STRONG><U>
We offer multiple purchase discounts – some of the items post for
free when combined with other purchases so please take the time to
browse our store
</U></STRONG></FONT></P>
```

Now that you have this code in place it is simply a matter of
changing the editable sections to suit your requirements for
each listing.

This editing can be carried out in the code, or in the listings
builder. You can also use the builder to change the colours and
fonts of the text to suit your shop theme.

SELLING FORMAT SECTION

In this section of the template you can set your format, listing duration and pricing.

In the procedure described here, we will assume that you wish to sell quantities of a single item over a long period:

1. Select 'Fixed Price' from the dropdown menu
2. Enter a price if required. If most of the items you intend to sell using this template have the same retail price insert it here; you can edit it during the listing process if required
3. Enter a quantity if required. The 'Quantity' of items you are listing will probably change so it is best to leave this field blank. If you are intending to order the same quantity of every item you intend to list using this template enter that figure here
4. Set the duration to 'GTC'. Any listings completed using this template will automatically relist when the listing expires until the items have sold out, at which point the listing will end. This allows you effectively to set your listing running and forget about it
5. Enter the VAT rate applicable to the item. If you are VAT registered and the items you intend to list using this template require VAT to be charged, you should enter the relevant rate in the VAT field. If you are not VAT registered leave this field blank

LISTING UPGRADES

Check the boxes for the listing upgrades if required (see the eBay help pages for more information on upgrades). Only check these boxes if you have factored the extra costs of these upgrades into your profit/loss figures for the items you intend to sell using this template. The eBay categories for 'Home and Garden' and 'Clothes, Shoes, and Accessories' offer the 'Gallery Plus' and 'Picture Pack' upgrades for free, so it is a simpler process to check the boxes to specify these options now if you are selling in these categories.

 Tip

Listing upgrades will increase the exposure of your item, making it more visible to your buyer.

POSTAGE OPTIONS

Now, go down to postage options. Here we can set up our postal charges for our 'Large Letter' template. If this template was going to be used for creating listings for 'Collection only' or 'Heavy & Bulky' items, we would select that option from the first dropdown menu. Details relating to the collection and delivery options for this selection would need to be added to the item description, and we would skip this section.

If you have decided to offer 'Free postage' on your economy service:

1. Select 2nd Class Standard from the dropdown menu
2. Click into the adjacent checkbox to select 'Free shipping'. It is preferable to offer more than one postal option, so in the next field:
3. Select Royal Mail 1st Class Standard from the dropdown menu
4. Enter the price you wish to charge for this service
5. Enter the price you would like to charge for the P&P of each additional item purchased
6. Select Royal Mail special Delivery (TM)

7. Enter the price you wish to charge for this service
8. Enter the price you would like to charge for the P&P of each additional item purchased. For example:

2nd Class Standard – Free P&P
1st Class Standard – £0.99 + £0.59
Recorded Delivery – £5.99 + £0.59

If you have decided to charge for postage across the range of services, complete the steps as detailed above but replace the first two steps with the ones below:

1. Select 2nd Class Standard from the dropdown menu
2. Enter the price you wish to charge for this service
3. Enter the price you would like to charge for the P&P of each additional item purchased. For example:

2nd Class Standard – £0.99 + £0.59
1st Class Standard – £1.39 + £0.59
Recorded Delivery – £6.99 + £0.59

If your items are high value, we would recommend sending them by recorded post and amend the options in the menu to reflect this change of service level.

If you would like to offer combined purchase discounts for your items (i.e. P&P discounts for multiple purchases) it is possible to set these up to apply automatically. This is another reason why we chose to organise our templates in this way:

1. Click the 'Create rules' link, beneath the 'Combined Postage Discounts' subheading. This opens internet explorer and allows you to create your postage rules in eBay
2. Click 'Create', under the heading 'Flat-rate postage rule'

3. Select 'Add an amount for each additional item'
4. Select 'Add profiles (Advanced)'
5. Enter the price as listed in your template for each additional item
6. Name this rule 'Large Letters'

This rule will now be applied to all items created using the 'Large Letter' template and will save you vast amounts of time when customers purchase multiple items from you. You will not need to amend any invoices yourself: it will all be done for you.

While you are here use the same process to create a few more rules and name them Package 1, Package 2, Courier 1, Courier 2, and Free. For example:

Large Letter – £0.59
Package 1 – £0.99
Package 2 – £1.49
Courier 1 – £1.99
Courier 2 – £2.99
Free – Check the 'Free P&P' checkbox

These other rules can then be applied to the templates you create for the larger packages.

If you are willing to allow buyers to collect their purchases from you:

1. Check the 'Local pickup' checkbox
2. Enter a flat rate charge for this service if required

It is widely accepted by eBay sellers that this service is supplied free of charge and you risk alienating buyers if you charge for this service. If you are going to incur justifiable costs by offering this service explain the reason for the charge in your listing description.

Next, set your Domestic Despatch Time:

Select the appropriate period from the dropdown menu

Even though you may offer a same-day despatch service, the fastest option here is one working day. This is a promise to your customer that you will despatch the item no later than the next working day. Buyers appreciate a fast despatch time: they have made their purchase and they want their goods.

If you have decided to offer the Special Delivery option and are willing to adhere to a domestic despatch time of one working day:

1. Scroll to the bottom of the postage options section
2. Click on the 'Postage Options' button
3. Scroll to the bottom
4. Check the 'Get It Fast' checkbox

This will boost your exposure in the eBay search and give your buyers the opportunity to receive their item on a guaranteed next-day delivery service.

While this pop-up window is open:

1. Click the 'Locations' tab
2. Enter the postcode from which the item is despatched. This is useful for people searching for a local supplier from which to make their purchase
3. Check 'Save for future listings'
4. Click the 'OK' button

You can now repeat this process for International postage options if you require.

PAYMENT METHOD

Set your required payment methods that you would like to associate with this template.

Now repeat the process for your other package types: Letter, Packages and Courier Items. We will need these templates later when it comes to listing your items.

COMPILING A LISTING PROCEDURE

Many of the selections in this procedure for compiling a listing should default to your preset settings in accordance with the Turbo Lister set up and the individual templates you compiled in the last section. They are included in this process for the benefit of those who have chosen not to set up the defaults and templates as suggested earlier in the guide.

PHOTOS

1. Take your photos or download them from the internet
2. Upload your photos to your 'eBay items to list' file on your computer
3. Open the 'eBay items to list' file
4. Rotate the images to the correct orientation
5. Delete any photos you are unhappy with or do not require
6. View each image independently and crop and/or fix the images as required
7. Move any photos (that you are not intending to use as the main listing or variation photos) that you would like to include in the listing description to another file on your desktop titled 'Photobucket uploads'

8. Copy any photos that you intend to use as a main listing photo or variation photo, and also want to include in your listing description, to the same file
9. Open the 'Photobucket uploads' file
10. Resize your photos to the size you require for your listing
11. Open Photobucket in your browser
12. Log in
13. Click the green 'Upload' button
14. Select the album to which you wish to upload from the dropdown menu on the right-hand side
15. Click the 'Select photos and videos' button
16. Browse to locate and open the 'Photobucket uploads' file on your desktop
17. Select the photos to upload
18. Click 'Open'

Your photos are now all edited, in place and easy to find, and ready to add to your listings.

👍**Tip**

Take your items out of the packaging and display them effectively before taking your photographs.

LISTING

1. Launch Turbo Lister
2. Click on the template most suited to use with your intended listing
3. Click on the 'Item from Template' button
4. Select from the list the folder into which you would like to save the listing

5. Click the 'Okay' button
6. In the title and category section, insert your title and subtitle (if required)
7. Under the heading 'Category', click the 'Select' button, then the 'Search categories' tab
8. Enter a few keywords relating to the item
9. Click the 'Search' button
10. Select from the list the result most applicable to your item
11. Click the 'Done' button
12. Repeat the procedure for the second category if required (further fees apply)
13. Select the shop categories in which you would like your item to appear
14. Enter the barcode or other identifying product code in to 'UPC/EAN/ISBN/VIN' field
15. Proceed to the 'Details' section
16. If you are listing a single item or product without variations, proceed to step 39.
17. If you have a variety of items you wish to sell on this single listing, click the 'Create Variations' button
18. Click the 'Add your own Variation Detail' button
19. Type the variation into the field (e.g. Colour, Size)
20. Click into the box below 'Enter Detail Name' and start to list your variations, each time clicking into the box below the last to add another (e.g. Small, Medium, Large)
21. Click the 'Next' button
22. Complete the 'Item Specifics' form with details relating to the item you are listing. If there are no suggestions click the 'get suggestions' button at the bottom left or create your own item specifics if required
23. Click the 'Next' button

24. Click the 'Create Variations' button
25. Enter the quantity and sale price next to each variation
26. Click the 'Next' button
27. Click into the frame under the heading 'Shared Pictures'
28. Select desktop
29. Browse and locate your 'eBay items to list' file
30. Open the file
31. Choose the photo you wish to use as the main listing photo for this item
32. Click the 'Insert' button
33. Repeat steps 27 to 32 to add photos to each of the variations
34. Click the 'Next' button
35. Confirm that the variations, quantities and prices are correct
36. Click the 'Done' button
37. Select the condition of the items from the dropdown menu
38. Proceed to the 'Pictures and Description' section and skip to step 50
39. Click the 'Edit' button next to 'Item Specifics'
40. Complete the 'Item Specifics' form as they relate to the item you are listing (if there are no suggestions click the 'get suggestions' button at the bottom left or create your own item specifics if required)
41. Click the 'Next' button
42. Select the condition of the items from the dropdown menu

👍**Tip**

At the end of a seasonal listing, wish your customers a Merry Christmas and Happy New Year, Happy Easter, Halloween, etc.

---

43. Proceed to the 'Pictures and Description' section
44. Click into the frame beneath the 'Pictures' heading
45. Select desktop
46. Browse and locate your 'eBay items to list' file
47. Open the file and choose the photo you wish to use as the main listing photo for this item
48. Click the 'Insert' button
49. Repeat steps 44 to 48 to add any other photos you would like to add to the listing (fees may apply in some categories)
50. Click the 'Description Builder' button
51. Change the asterixed sections of text to add your title, description and features fields to your description template
52. Click the 'Save' button
53. Open another tab in your browser
54. Navigate to Photobucket
55. Log in
56. Navigate to the album containing the photos that you would like to include in the description
57. Roll your mouse over the photo of your choice
58. Click on the code marked 'HTML Code'
59. Paste the code in place of the '***REPLACE WITH LINKS TO PHOTOBUCKET***' code in Turbo Lister. If you have more than one photo repeat steps 57 to 59 for each photo you want to insert. Ensure that you allow a space between the pieces of pasted code to allow the photos to distribute themselves appropriately in the listing
60. Proceed to the 'Selling Format' section
61. If you created variations on your listing skip to step 65
62. Select your selling format from the dropdown menu
63. Enter your price
64. Select the 'Duration' of your listing from the dropdown menu

65. Proceed to the 'Listing Upgrades' section
66. If you are listing your items in the 'Home and Garden' or 'Clothes, Shoes, and Accessories' categories, check the boxes next to 'Gallery Plus' and 'Picture Pack': they are free. If you are not listing your items in these categories there will be an extra fee for these upgrades
67. Proceed to the 'Postage Options' section
68. Select the postage type from the dropdown menu
69. Specify your 'Domestic Services' options and prices
70. Click the checkbox if you would like to allow customers to collect the item from you
71. Specify the charge for doing so if necessary
72. Specify the combined postage discount that applies to your listing (if you have set this up)
73. Check to apply your promotional shipping rule (if you have set this up), if applicable
74. Select your 'Domestic Despatch Time' from the dropdown menu
75. Proceed to 'Payment Methods'
76. Check that the details are correct
77. Click on the 'Save' button at the bottom right-hand side of the screen
78. Locate your newly completed listing in the Turbo Lister file
79. Click to highlight it
80. Click the 'Add to upload' button
81. If you have further items to list return to step 10; if you have finished listing your items proceed to step 82
82. Click on the 'Waiting to upload' button on the left-hand side of the page
83. Click the 'Upload all' button

84. Turbo Lister will calculate the fees: check that the fees are as expected. If they are high, you will need to disable some of the 'Listing upgrades' specified at step 66

85. Click the 'Upload Now' button

👍 **Tip**

Organise your photos into Windows and Photobucket folders – it will save you lots of time when you need to find them again.

5
MANAGING YOUR SALES

INVOICING YOUR CUSTOMERS

This task should become part of your daily routine.

Some eBay members prefer to be sent an invoice prior to sending their payment, particularly if they are making multiple purchases from you. It gives you a chance to add a further discount as a thank you or loyalty reward.

SENDING AN INVOICE

1. Open eBay in your browser
2. Log in to your account
3. From the SMP Summary page, click the 'Awaiting Payment' link in the navigation bar on the left-hand side of the page. You will be presented with a menu showing all of the transactions for which you are awaiting payment
4. Click the 'Send Invoice' link on the right-hand side of the transaction details under the heading 'Actions'. This will display the invoice. Here you can amend the details such as:
   P&P service level – if your customer has requested a service level that is not available on the listing you can

amend the details here; you can also add or remove postal services from the invoice

Seller's discount – if you have agreed a discount or extra charge with your customer enter it here

Personal message – if there is something that you need to communicate to your buyer prior to them sending payment this is your opportunity. It is a good idea to supply your terms and conditions of sale or info regarding upgrading their P&P choice. For example:

Many thanks for your purchase. If you would like to upgrade the postal service of your item(s) from the Economy (2nd Class Post) 3–5 day (may take up to 14 days) service to either the Standard (1st Class Post) 1–2 day (may take up to 5 days) service or Get It Fast (Special Delivery) guaranteed next working day services please let me know prior to sending your payment.

Please don't hesitate to contact me if I can assist in any way.

5. Click the 'Send Invoice' button

UNPAID INVOICES

eBay will send a reminder to your buyers if payment has not been received within forty-eight hours of you sending an invoice. Some buyers will ignore this email as spam or forget to deal with it. We recommend allowing your buyer five days from the invoice date before sending a further reminder to them. For example:

POLITE REMINDER

Hi,

It has been 5 days since you made a commitment to purchase this item and I haven't received payment.

If you would like to proceed with the transaction please send payment as soon as you can. If you would prefer to cancel the order please let me know and I can process the request.

If I do not receive payment or a response to this message within 48 hours I will open an unpaid item dispute.

If you have any questions or queries please do not hesitate to contact me, I am pleased to help in any way I can.

To send this message:

1. Navigate to the 'Awaiting Payment' page
2. Click 'More actions'
3. Select 'Contact buyer' from the dropdown menu
4. Type your message
5. Click the 'Send' button

More often than not, once you have sent this reminder you will receive payment along with an apologetic message.

If you have not received payment within forty-eight hours of sending the reminder you will need to open an 'Unpaid Item Dispute'.

UNPAID ITEM DISPUTE

The process involved in opening an Unpaid Item Dispute is covered in the 'Using the Resolution Centre' section of Chapter 7.

AMENDING THE DELIVERY ADDRESS

If a buyer requests that you amend the delivery address for any reason, it is best to do it on the eBay system. This will keep the change as a permanent amendment and will serve as proof of the address to which you despatched the item should something go awry.

To amend the address:

1. Navigate to the 'Awaiting payment' or 'Awaiting postage' screen
2. Locate the transaction that requires the amendment

3. Click the 'View sales record' link in the dropdown menu under the 'Actions' heading
4. Amend the address as required by clicking into the relevant fields
5. Scroll down the page
6. Click the 'Save' button

👍**Tip**

Only use the Resolution Centre as a last resort – try to resolve things amicably to ensure your buyer doesn't feel bullied.

👍**Tip**

Invoice your buyer as soon as you can after they make their purchase – prompt responses are always appreciated.

PRINTING YOUR DESPATCH NOTES

One of the advantages of using the Selling Manager Pro system is that you are provided with a printable combined address label and invoice/packing slip, which also provides a return address within the same field. If you combine using this template with an A4 integrated label it means you need only print one sheet per order. Utilising this provision supplies your customers with an invoice and you with an address label. If you have an online business account with the Royal Mail you can also print your postage impression direct to the label, again saving time and money.

SETTING UP YOUR DESPATCH LABEL

From the Selling Manager Pro Summary page:

1. Click on the 'Awaiting Postage' link in the navigation bar on the left-hand side of the screen. This will bring up a list of all the transactions for which payment has been received and items that are awaiting despatch

2. Click the checkbox at the top of the left-hand column. This will check the boxes next to all of the transactions listed

3. Click the 'Despatch action' button

4. Select 'Print postage labels or invoices'

5. Click the link at the bottom to 'Edit invoice & address label template'

6. Edit your return address. This should default to the address you supplied on your account. If you despatch from a different address you can amend it now

7. Add your phone number to the postage label by checking this box. We recommend that you don't display your phone number to prevent unwanted direct contact from customers or third parties

8. Add your web address. If you have an independent website or wish to supply the web address of your eBay shop, you can enter the details here

9. Add buyer information. You can choose to add some of the customer's contact details to the document. We recommend adding the buyer's email address and phone number to the invoice. This occasionally comes in useful if there is a problem with the order as it saves time having to go into the transaction details to find the information. We also recommend that you don't add the buyer's phone number to the postage label as your customer may receive unwanted calls from third parties

10. Show gallery image. This will add a small thumbnail image of the item to the invoice

11. Seller logo for invoice. If you have uploaded or selected a logo for your shop select the button to 'Use your shop logo'; this gives the document a professionally branded appearance

12. Personal message. Add a personal message at the bottom of your invoice to further communicate with your buyer. Try something like:

> We hope you are very happy with your purchase. If for any reason you are displeased, please contact us through the eBay messaging system. We are always very happy to assist in any way we can. Please remember to leave feedback and star ratings so that others can see how well we perform.

13. Click the 'Save' button

 Tip
Use S7 (aka G or 3) type integrated labels for your address label/ packing slip to speed up your despatch process.

PRINTING YOUR DESPATCH LABELS

Now that your template is set up:

1. Under the heading 'Invoice and Address Labels' select 'Address labels & invoice/packing slip'

2. Click the 'Continue' button. A new window will pop-up with your invoice/packing slips ready to print

3. Print the labels as you would normally print any document from your browser

If you find that the documents are printing with headers and footers and you would like to remove them, go to the eBay 'Print postage labels' page, where you will find a small tip box which says, 'Learn how to remove extra information from the top and bottom of your printouts'. Click the link and follow the instructions contained within to eradicate the information from your document.

The next time you print your despatch notes you will not need to edit your template: the settings will be saved.

CHANGING THE DESPATCH STATUS

Now you have printed the labels you need to mark the items as despatched. This clears them from the 'Awaiting Despatch' menu and places them in the 'Paid and Despatch' menu. It is very important that this procedure is followed to prevent despatching items twice. To do this:

1. Click the 'Back' link next to the 'Continue' button on the 'Print postage labels' page
2. Check the box at the top of the left-hand column to check all of the transactions as before
3. Click the 'Change Status' button
4. Select 'Despatched' from the dropdown menu
5. Click the 'Confirm' button

If you have courier items to despatch don't change their status to 'despatched' yet. If you change the status now, the Parcel2Go integration system will not locate them. Open Parcel2Go and arrange their despatch (see the 'Using Parcel2Go Integration' section in Chapter 6) before marking them as despatched.

PRINTED POSTAGE IMPRESSION (PPI)

If you have a Royal Mail Online Business Account, the final stage is to add your PPI to your label. Sort your labels into piles for 1st Class, 2nd Class and Other. Only 1st and 2nd Class post require PPIs; special deliveries and international services just require the self-adhesive label, and any courier consignments will have their own label.

Count your 1st Class labels and place them in your printer. Locate your '1st Class PPI' document and open it. Print the amount required.

Repeat the process for your 2nd Class labels.

Now you're ready to start packing.

DESPATCH PROCEDURE

Follow the steps below:

1. Go to SMP Summary
2. Click on the 'Awaiting Postage' link
3. Check the box at the top of the left-hand column
4. Click the 'Despatch action' button
5. Select 'Print postage labels or invoices'
6. Select 'Address labels & invoice/packing slip'
7. Click the 'Continue' button
8. Print from your browser in the pop-up window
9. Click the 'Back' link, next to the 'Continue' button on the 'Print postage labels' page
10. Check the box at the top of the left-hand column
11. Click the 'Change Status' button
12. Click 'Despatched'
13. Click 'Confirm'
14. Return to step 3 and repeat the process until all orders are despatched
15. Sort your labels by service level
16. Print your 1st Class PPIs
17. Print your 2nd Class PPIs

SELLING MANAGER PRO SUMMARY

This helpful page will provide you with lots of information about the current state of your business. If you followed my advice earlier in the guide you will have already set this page as your web browser's home page.

Take some time to explore the many windows and links embedded into the page: they will give you fast access to information and tasks you will need to complete on a daily basis, most notably:

'At a glance': a bar chart displaying your daily, weekly, monthly and quarterly sales revenue

'Seller Dashboard Summary': how you are performing as an eBay seller

'Sold': statistics and links to your sales transactions in their different statuses. Use these links to navigate to your sales awaiting payment, sales awaiting dispatch and completed transactions. Also there is a link to the Resolution Centre and statistics and information relating to any open cases

'Listing activity': statistics and links to your active listings, scheduled listings and ended listings. Of particular interest in this field is the ended listings section, and in particular the 'Sold' link. Clicking this link will open a menu displaying all of the listings that have ended because your stock has run out; a glance at this should be incorporated into your daily schedule so that you can make a note and reorder the expired stock

ESTABLISHING A DAILY ROUTINE

It is important that you have a daily and weekly routine to add some structure to your working day. Depending on the service levels you have offered customers you may have deadlines or commitments to fulfil. We recommend structuring your day something like this:

08:00 – Check and respond to your messages
08:30 – Send invoices for any unpaid items
08:45 – Print despatch orders received after close of despatch deadline on Friday
09:00 – Pack your items ready for despatch
14:00 – Print despatch orders at close of despatch deadline
14:15 – Pack items ready for despatch
15:30 – Sort and count packages into bags and weigh
15:45 – Complete order with RMOBA
16:00 – Tag bags ready for collection or delivery to mail centre

The gap between finishing the packing of the first batch of items and printing your final despatch orders for that day at 14:00 is the time you should schedule for your research, photography and listings. It is advisable to spread these tasks over the working week. For example:

Monday – Your busiest packing day: all orders placed after your despatch deadline on the previous Friday will be awaiting despatch
Tuesday – Research new items to sell
Wednesday – Photograph, edit, and upload images of new items ready for listing
Thursday – Compile and upload listings for new items
Friday – Check your competition and adjust your active listings
Saturday and Sunday – Limit your activity to responding to customer queries and have a well-earned rest

---

👆**Tip**

Be strict with yourself and ensure you turn up for work on time.
Don't be tempted to slack off: your business needs you to run it.

REFUNDING A BUYER

On occasion you will find it necessary to issue a refund to your buyer. The process is the same for a partial refund or a full refund.

You will not receive a Final Value Fee credit from eBay for a partial refund, for refunds issued outside of the resolution centre or for purchases that were made more than forty-five days previously.

BEFORE ISSUING A REFUND

Before you decide to issue a refund, there are a few checks you should make:

1. The date of purchase: if the buyer received the item more than seven days previously you are not obliged to issue a refund or accept a return. If the item was purchased more than forty-five days previously, you will not be entitled to a Final Value Fee credit from eBay. If the item was purchased more than sixty days previously the buyer will not be able to leave feedback for you

2. Feedback: if the buyer has left positive feedback, they cannot leave negative feedback. An eBay member can only ever amend feedback by obtaining permission from the other member to do so or by receiving a request from the other member to amend the feedback

ISSUING THE REFUND

If you have made the checks detailed above and have decided to issue a refund, follow the steps below:

1. Navigate to the SMP Summary page
2. Click the 'Sold' link in the navigation bar on the left-hand side
3. Use the search function to locate the transaction you need to refund
4. From the dropdown menu located on the right-hand side of the transaction, under the heading 'Action', select 'View sales record'
5. Scroll down the page, locate the 'Payment information' and click the link to view the 'PayPal transaction details'
6. Log in to your PayPal account (if necessary)
7. Scroll down the transaction details and click the link to 'Issue a refund'
8. Enter the amount you wish to refund, the transaction reference or invoice number and a short message to the buyer
9. Click the 'Continue' button
10. Confirm the refund by clicking the 'Issue refund' button

RECLAIMING YOUR EBAY FEES

eBay will credit the Final Value Fees for a transaction in which you refunded the buyer in full. In order to reclaim your eBay fees for the transaction you need to open a cancellation case in the Resolution Centre. The procedure for this is covered in the 'Using the Resolution Centre' section of Chapter 7.

USING HOLIDAY SETTINGS

When this mode is activated eBay will display a user-customisable message in your listings so that you can let your buyers know that you are closed, explain why and tell them when you will reopen. It is also possible to add a customised message to your shop-front.

ACTIVE OR INACTIVE?

You will need to decide whether you want to keep your listings active so that buyers can continue to make purchases from you while you're away. If you don't, you can turn off your listings so that buyers are unable to complete the purchase and will need to wait until your return in order to buy the item. Both of these options have their drawbacks.

Keeping your listings active will mean that buyers will have to wait until you return before the item is despatched. By choosing this option you risk the possibility of receiving neutral or negative feedback and low despatch time DSRs (Detailed Seller Ratings) from buyers who have not read your message properly, or have not understood the concept that the shop is on holiday settings.

The alternative is to make your listings inactive. By choosing this option your buyer will still be able to find your item in the search results but will be informed that they are unable to complete their purchase until your return. The result of choosing this option is that you will probably lose sales, but you will not leave yourself exposed to the possibility of receiving negative or neutral feedback.

Having tried both options in the past, we would recommend that you choose the second option and deactivate your listings. Maintaining a high feedback score is crucial to the reputation of your business and future sales.

ACTIVATING THE HOLIDAY SETTINGS

Follow the steps below to activate your holiday settings:

1. Launch your browser
2. Login to your eBay account
3. Scroll down the page to the 'Manage my shop' field
4. Click on the 'Holiday settings' link
5. Check the box to turn on your out-of-office email response if required. If it is not required, leave the box empty and proceed to step 9
6. Enter the start date
7. Enter the end date
8. Type your auto response into the field. For example:

Dear Valued Customer, Thank you for trying to contact us. Unfortunately, we are currently closed for business. Our shop will reopen on ***ENTER DATE*** and we will respond to your query as soon as possible.

👍 Tip

The auto-response for eBay messages can be used independently of the holiday settings – useful if you are away for the weekend.

---

9. Check the box to turn on your shop holiday settings
10. If you have chosen to make your listings inactive check the box to 'Hide and block purchases of my fixed price listings'. If you prefer to keep your listings active leave the box empty and proceed to step 15
11. Check the box to 'Display a return date' if you know the date your business will reopen. If you do not know when you will be able to reopen, proceed to step 20
12. Enter the date or select the date from the calendar
13. Type a message to your buyers into the field. For example:

Dear Valued Customer, Please accept our sincere apologies, but we are currently closed for business. Our shop will reopen on ***ENTER DATE*** when our normal service will resume.

14. Proceed to step 20
15. Check the box to 'Display a return date'
16. Enter the date or select the date from the calendar
17. Type a message to your buyers into the field. For example:

Dear Valued Customer, We are currently closed for business. Our shop will reopen on ***ENTER DATE*** when our normal service will resume. Any orders placed between ***ENTER DATE*** and *** ENTER DATE*** will not be despatched until *** ENTER DATE***. Please accept our sincere apologies for any inconvenience caused.

18. Proceed to step 20
19. Type a message to your buyers into the field. For example:

Dear Valued Customer, Please accept our sincere apologies, but we are currently closed for business. At this present time we are unable to provide you with any information regarding our reopening date, but please add us to your favourite seller's list … We'll be back soon.

20. Click the 'Apply' button

 Tip
Don't be tempted to leave listings active while you're away –
someone will leave you a negative feedback or low DSRs.

6
DESPATCHING YOUR ITEMS

PACKING YOUR ITEMS

DECIDING HOW TO PACK YOUR ITEM

The first question to be asked when packing your item is 'How much protection does it need?' The postal system is brutal, and your item will be exposed to knocks, abrasion, vibration and crushing. All of these factors should be considered when deciding how to pack your item.

We recommend applying the 'Football' rule: if you are confident that kicking the package across the room like a football will not damage it, then it will probably survive the postal system.

PACKAGING TYPES

The packaging required will vary from item to item, but we have found that a selection of envelopes, self-sealing mailing bags, bubble wrap and cardboard boxes will cater for 99 per cent of the items despatched by post.

Envelopes

The largest envelope size that can be sent under the letter category with the Royal Mail is C5; the largest that can be sent as a large letter is C4. Envelopes are suitable for posting photos, postcards, CDs, DVDs, magazines and suchlike. We recommend holding a stock of both of these sizes for posting items and business mail.

Self-sealing mailing bags

These are fantastic for all types of items: quick to use, durable and water resistant, these bags are used by all the major catalogues as a cost-effective way of packing a wide variety of items. They are available in many sizes, shapes and colours. We recommend holding a stock of up to five different sizes across the range depending on your requirements.

Bubble wrap

This is a good way to protect some fragile items; if your product range has breakables then this product is an essential purchase. There are two types of wrap: large bubble or small bubble. Large bubble wraps are better suited to wrapping more delicate items as they provide more of a cushioning effect, but the wrap itself is also more delicate so it should be used within a box. This product is also better for void filling. Small bubble wrap is more durable so is better for items that do not require a cardboard box but still require some level of cushioning effect.

👍 **Tip**

When sourcing a packaging supplier, don't always go for the cheapest – sometimes paying a little extra is worth it for a better service. Adhesives and odours can vary from supplier to supplier. Clothing should be sent in odourless packaging.

Cardboard boxes

The best way to pack your fragile items is to use a combination of bubble wrap and cardboard; it's the only way to get your really fragile items to the customer in one piece. Boxes are available in many different sizes: take a look at the range of products you need to send in boxes before deciding on the sizes you require. Remember that on occasion you may need to send two or three of the same item to a customer.

We recommend keeping a stock of two or three different sizes of carton. You can also recycle the boxes in which you receive your stock.

TAPE

Don't be tempted to purchase cheap tape: you end up using more, so it ends up costing you both time and money. Good-quality tape can be obtained from packaging suppliers for less than you would pay for the cheaper tapes on the high street. Be careful when making your purchase: some rolls are cheaper because they carry less tape. Compare the prices on a cost per metre basis.

One-inch clear tape

Use this for sticking your envelopes closed and sticking your address labels to your packages.

Tip

Negotiate an exclusive deal with your packaging supplier: you will receive huge discounts across their range.

Two-inch packing tape

Used for taping boxes shut. The low-noise varieties generally have a better adhesive than the alternatives.

Two-inch fragile tape

Used for clearly marking your parcels 'FRAGILE'. Source the cheapest you can find: you won't use much of it as the fragile tape is only used for marking purposes rather than being used to seal a package.

Tip

Recycle any packaging you receive from your suppliers. Keep bubble wrap and flatten boxes down to store them. This will save you heaps of space and money, and it's very good for the environment too!

COMPLIMENT SLIPS

It is a good idea to enclose a compliment slip with every item you despatch. It works as a reminder to your buyer that you are there to assist them with any problems they may have with the item, and it directs them to contact you regarding the issue before resorting to leaving negative feedback or opening a dispute case.

Spend a little time using a word-processing program such as Word to compile a professional-looking compliment slip that features your logo and a set of instructions. You can get multiple quantities of these to fit on a single sheet of A4 and print them out when required. Here's a sample text:

> Thank you for your purchase. If you have any queries or concerns about the item you have received, please contact us through the eBay messaging system. We guarantee a response within 24 hours Monday to Friday. Please remember that we are committed to offering you a 5-star customer service and are here to help you resolve any issues before you leave feedback.

 Tip

Consider your costs before choosing coloured bags or glossy packaging – does your buyer really care?

CHOOSING POSTAL OPTIONS

ROYAL MAIL

The Royal Mail is probably going to receive approximately 90 per cent of your business. It can provide several variations of service levels to meet all of your postal requirements.

The most popular UK services used by eBay traders are 1st and 2nd Class Post, Recorded Signed For and Special Deliveries.

1st Class

Items are generally delivered on the next working day, including Saturdays, but this is not guaranteed.

2nd Class

Items are generally delivered within three working days, but may take up to fifteen working days.

Recorded Signed For

This provides a proof of delivery for 1st and 2nd Class mail at a fixed extra charge.

Special Delivery

This provides a guaranteed next day delivery to 99 per cent of the UK with proof of delivery, up to £2,500 compensation and online tracking.

PACKAGE TYPES

Letters

Useful for greeting cards, personal letters, postcards and items that fit into C5 envelopes.

Letter dimensions:
Length: 240 mm max
Width: 165 mm max
Thickness: 5 mm max
Weight: 100 g max

Large letters

Useful for A4 documents, CDs and DVDs in their cases, some large greeting cards, most magazines and other items that fit into C4 envelopes.

Large letter dimensions:
Length: 353 mm max
Width: 250 mm max
Thickness: 25 mm max
Weight: 750 g max

Tip

Try to send more items in letter format – sometimes items can be removed from their packaging allowing them to be sent as a letter. This will save on costs, giving you an edge over the competition.

Packets

Useful for clothes, shoes, posters and books.

Packet dimensions:

Size: 610 mm x 460 mm x 460 mm max

Size for posters or other rolled items: 900 mm max length. The length plus twice the diameter must be no more than 1,040 mm.

Weight: no weight limit for items sent 1st Class. 2nd Class items must be under 1,000 g (increases to 2,000 g if you have subscribed to either the Packetpost or Packetsort option)

Parcels

If your item is over the maximum size or weight for the packet format, you will need to send it as a 'Parcel' with Royal Mail Standard Parcels, Parcelforce Worldwide or another carrier.

Parcel dimensions:

Size: 1.5 m length max; length/girth combined 3 m max

Weight: 20 kg max (Royal Mail) or 30 kg max (Parcelforce Worldwide)

Tip

Use couriers when cost effective: your product will be tracked and insured, and you will receive proof of delivery.

PARCEL2GO

This is a one-stop shop for door-to-door courier services. Parcel2Go will be able to provide you with the service you require to deliver items ranging from small packages up to full pallets, in the UK and worldwide, at a competitive price. It offers a selection of service levels, using a variety of suppliers.

Parcel2Go suppliers

City Link
Fedex
Parcelforce
Palletforce
UPS
TNT
Hermes
Yodel

Services

Parcel2Go offers a wide range of services to cater for all your requirements. All services obtain a proof of delivery, and are fully insured and tracked. A 'Live Help' service is available for any queries or questions relating to your consignment. Terms and conditions vary from carrier to carrier.

Tip
There are various ways of obtaining a discount from Parcel2Go
– visit the website for details.

DECIDING WHICH CARRIER TO USE

If you have set up your Royal Mail Online Business Account
(RMOBA) and Parcel2Go account, your choices are going to
be relatively straightforward. More often than not, the service
you choose will be dictated by the buyer, but this decision
process should also be used when deciding what service levels
and parcel carriers to offer when listing your item:

1. Will the item post as a letter?
   Yes – Proceed to 2
   No – Proceed to 7
2. Do you require a proof of delivery?
   Yes – Proceed to 3
   No – Proceed to 5
3. Is it urgent?
   Yes – Proceed to 4
   No – Send your item by Royal Mail 2nd Class Recorded
   Post
4. Do you require a next day delivery?
   Yes – Send your item by Royal Mail Special Delivery
   No – Send your item by Royal Mail 1st Class Recorded
   Post
5. Is it urgent?
   Yes – Proceed to 6
   No – Post your item by Royal Mail 2nd Class Post

6. Do you require a next day delivery?

   Yes – Send your item by Royal Mail Special Delivery

   No – Send your item by Royal Mail 1st Class Post

7. Will the item post as a package?

   Yes – Proceed to 8

   No – Proceed to 11

8. Do you require a proof of delivery?

   Yes – Proceed to 9

   No – Proceed to 13

9. Is it urgent?

   Yes – Proceed to 10

   No – Compare 2nd Class Recorded prices with economy options from Parcel2Go

10. Do you require next-day delivery?

    Yes – Compare Special Delivery prices with next-day options from Parcel2Go

    No – Compare 1st Class Recorded prices with express options from Parcel2Go

---

👍 Tip

Offer a minimum of 1st Class, 2nd Class and Special Delivery on all of your listings – some buyers will pay extra to get their item faster.

---

11. Is it urgent?

    Yes – Proceed to 12

    No – Book an economy service with Parcel2Go

12. Do you require next-day delivery?

    Yes – Book a next-day service with Parcel2Go

    No – Book an express service with Parcel2Go

13. Is it urgent?

    Yes – Proceed to 14

    No – Compare 2nd Class prices with economy services from Parcel2Go

14. Do you require a next day delivery?

    Yes – Compare Special Delivery prices with next-day options from Parcel2Go

    No – Compare 1st Class prices with express options from Parcel2Go

---

 Tip

Don't overcharge your buyer for P&P – you will receive low DSRs.

USING RMOBA

The first time you use your Royal Mail Online Business Account you will receive instruction over the telephone with a specialist from the Royal Mail. We have provided this information as a guide for reference after your training session has ended. Skip to the sections you require.

PRODUCT CODES

STL – Standard Tariff Letters applies to letters only

CRL – Packetpost Daily Rate applies to large letters and packets including Recorded Signed For

SD1 – Special Delivery 1 p.m.

OLA – International post including Airsure and International Signed For

COMPILING AN ORDER

This tutorial covers the steps required to send the most common types of post sent with RMOBA. We are using an example of a typical order but our order may not match our example; use the steps you require and ignore the ones you don't require.

Login

1. Launch your browser
2. Navigate to the URL: https://www.royalmail.com/discounts-payment/credit-account/online-business-account
3. Login

Create an order

4. Click the button to 'Access Online Business Account'
5. Click the 'Your accounts' link
6. Click the link to 'Create new order'

Number of services utilised

7. A field is required for each service you need; the default is 5. If you require more, select the quantity from the dropdown menu in the bottom left corner
8. Click the 'Update order' button

Product codes

9. Insert the relevant product code into each field for each service that you are sending that day
10. Click the 'Update order' button
11. If you have STL orders to despatch proceed to step 12; if not, skip to step 20

Details (STL)

12. Click the 'Details' button next to the STL order
13. Select the class
14. Select the format 'Letter'
15. Enter the quantity of letters
16. Enter the average weight
17. If the item is being sent as recorded, select 'Recorded' from the dropdown menu
18. Click the 'Accept' button
19. Repeat until all STL details are completed
20. If you have CRL items to despatch proceed to step 21; if not, skip to step 30

Details (CRL)

21. Click the 'Details' button next to the CRL order
22. Select 01 from the dropdown menu
23. Select the class
24. Select the format
25. Enter the quantity of items
26. Enter the average weight
27. If the item is being sent as recorded, select 'Recorded' from the dropdown menu
28. Click the 'Accept' button
29. Repeat until all CRL details are completed
30. If you have SD1 items to despatch proceed to step 31, if not skip to step 36

Details (SD1)

31. Click the 'Details' button next to the SD1 order
32. Enter the quantity of items being sent in the relevant weight category

33. Click the 'Accept' button
34. Repeat until all CRL details are completed
35. If you have OLA items to despatch proceed to step 36; if not, skip to step 44

Details (OLA)

36. Click the 'Details' button next to the OLA order
37. Select the region from the dropdown menu
38. Select the format from the dropdown menu
39. Select the country description from the dropdown menu
40. Enter the number of items
41. Enter the average weight
42. Select the priority service fee from the dropdown menu
43. Click the 'Accept' button

Confirm order

44. Click the 'Confirm order' button
45. Click the 'Okay' button

Print order

46. Scroll to the bottom of the pop-up window
47. Click the 'Print' button
48. Change the quantity to 2
49. Click the 'Print' button

 Tip
Have the same login details for all of the accounts you set up – it makes them much easier to remember.

USING PARCEL2GO INTEGRATION

The Parcel2Go integration system is an excellent time-saving despatch tool. It will import the order details from eBay making the despatch of your courier items faster and easier. Hopefully you will have already set up your account as described earlier in the guide. The integration system is very easy to use:

1. Launch your browser
2. Type in the following URL: www.parcel2go.com
3. Click the 'Go to my account' button on the right-hand side of the screen
4. Click the 'Integration' tab
5. Click the 'Item management' link under the heading 'eBay Item Shipping'
6. Enter your login details
7. Click the 'Login' button
8. Click the 'Item management' link again
9. Click the 'Download Items' button
10. Scroll down the page selecting the relevant service for each of the items you need to despatch
11. Check the boxes to the right-hand side of each shipment you wish to despatch
12. Scroll to the bottom of the screen
13. Click the 'Ship' button
14. Check that the details are correct
15. Click the 'Continue' button
16. Select your collection address from the dropdown menu and proceed to step 25. If your address does not appear in the menu, click the 'Add Address' button
17. Click the 'UK' button
18. Enter your postcode

19. Click the 'Find Address' button
20. Select your address from the dropdown menu
21. Click the 'Use Address' button
22. Complete the address details as required
23. Check the 'Is default address' box
24. Click the 'Submit' button
25. Enter your contact telephone number
26. Select your desired collection date from the dropdown menu
27. Enter your discount code if applicable
28. Click the 'Continue' button
29. Scroll down the page
30. Check the box to accept the terms and conditions
31. Click the 'Go to Checkout' button
32. Select your chosen payment method
33. Checkout in the manner appropriate to your payment method
34. Print your despatch label

DEALING WITH LOST OR DELAYED POST

In the event of a buyer contacting you to request knowledge of the whereabouts of their purchase, several steps should be taken before declaring the item 'Lost in the post'.

1. Has the item been paid for?
   Yes – Proceed to 2
   No – Inform the buyer that they have not yet paid for the item, and as soon as payment is received the item will be despatched
2. Was the item sent by a tracked or signed for service?
   Yes – Proceed to 3
   No – Proceed to 4

3. Has the item been delivered?

   Yes – Provide the buyer with the details supplied as a proof of delivery

   No – Provide the buyer with the tracking information relating to their item and the details required for them to continue tracking their item

4. Was the item sent by 2nd Class Post?

   Yes – Respond to the buyer with the 2nd Class Post sample response given in the 'Templates for communicating with your buyers' section of Chapter 7

   No – Proceed to 5

5. Respond to your buyer with the 1st Class Post sample response given in the 'Templates for communicating with your buyers' section of Chapter 7

👍 **Tip**

Be firm and adhere to your policies – the buyer accepted them when they made the purchase.

Hopefully this will have satisfied your buyer. If they contact you again after the period you have requested, stating that the item still has not been delivered, you will have no option but to issue a refund and submit a claim for loss with the relevant carrier.

👍 **Tip**

Exhaust all avenues of investigation before issuing a refund – the item may turn up later, and then you're out of pocket.

PROCESSING RETURNS AND DAMAGES

The returns policy we provided in the 'eBay customisable texts' section of Chapter 3 allows for fair treatment of your buyer and is also fair to you. You must ensure that you comply with the policy you provide to your buyer and the law. You must also ensure that the policy you provide complies with eBay's policies and the law.

DISTANCE SELLING REGULATIONS

The Distance Selling Regulations Act applies to most online sales; there are very few exceptions. Familiarise yourself with the Distance Selling Regulations as you will need to know that you are staying on the right side of the law.

There is a very useful leaflet that will give you a brief outline of the requirements your business needs to meet. It can be downloaded at: www.oft.gov.uk/shared_oft/business_leaflets/general/oft913.pdf

RETURNS

The most applicable parts of the Act for eBay sellers relate to the return of items.

The Act requires that you, as a seller, pay for the return of an item if the buyer wants to return it, unless you inform the buyer prior to purchase that they are liable for any costs involved in the return of the item.

Some sellers try to apply this exception to the rule across the board regardless of reason, but they will soon fall foul of the feedback system and the Resolution Centre. We recommend that you offer to pay for the return of damaged or faulty items. It is only fair, and you can often claim compensation from the carrier in return.

The Act also requires that you must allow your buyer seven days from the date they receive the item to assess it and contact you if they wish to return it (some items are exempt from this clause). If seven days have passed, you are not obliged to accept their request to return the item, but you must weigh up this option against receiving negative or neutral feedback.

Your buyer is responsible for the item until it is returned to you. You can claim compensation from your buyer for any damage the item sustains while in their care (although this right is very rarely pursued).

DAMAGES

If the buyer contacts you claiming that their item has arrived damaged, don't issue a refund immediately. Your carrier will require evidence of this damage before they will compensate you.

Ask the buyer to provide you with photos of:

1. The exterior of packaging
2. The interior of the packaging
3. The item
4. The damaged area

Some of the people who report damages are scammers and you will never hear from them again. If you do receive the photos from the buyer, assess the situation. Sometimes your buyer will be happy with a partial refund or a replacement item. Sometimes they will request a full refund.

It is up to you to decide whether to ask your buyer to return the item to you. If you have stated in your returns policy that you will reimburse buyers for the cost of returning damaged items you will need to decide if it makes financial sense to ask them to return it. If the item is repairable you may be able to sell it as repaired and recoup your losses. If you are going to have to discard the item, it is probably best to ask the buyer to dispose of it and save yourself the cost of the return postage.

Please take a look at the 'Templates for communicating with your buyers' section of Chapter 7 for examples of templates that you could use when dealing with these issues.

Tip

Ensure your returns policy complies with both eBay's policies and the Distance Selling Regulations.

7
PROVIDING AN AFTERSALES SERVICE

COMMUNICATING WITH YOUR BUYERS

Fast, amiable and polite responses to your customers' enquiries are essential to maintaining a high feedback score in the communication category of the Detailed Seller Ratings. There are many ways to communicate with your eBay customers:

EMAIL

We recommend that you set up a catch-all email address with one of the webmail providers to receive the notification emails from eBay and PayPal. Provide this email address to eBay as your contact email and set up an auto-response that provides the following reply to any emails received at that address:

> Many thanks for trying to contact us. Unfortunately, this email address is not monitored. Please redirect your communications via the eBay messaging system where we promise to respond to your query within 24 hours.
>
> Please accept our sincere apologies for any inconvenience.

This will ensure that any communications your customers direct to you will arrive via the eBay messaging system.

👍 **Tip**

Do not use your personal email for eBay: set up a webmail account for exclusive use by your business.

TELEPHONE

Unless you don't mind eBay customers phoning you at all times of the day or night, weekends or holidays, don't put your personal phone number on eBay.

We recommend purchasing a cheap 'Pay As You Go' phone for use as a dedicated eBay customer service number. This will allow you to set the phone to divert to voicemail when you don't want to receive calls. If you would prefer not to receive any calls, set your phone up to divert all calls and leave a message saying something like:

> Many thanks for trying to contact us. Unfortunately, this voicemail is not monitored. Please redirect your communications via the eBay messaging system where we promise to respond to your query within 24 hours. Please accept our sincere apologies for any inconvenience.

eBAY MESSAGING SYSTEM

The eBay messaging system is the most popular link between you and your customers. Most eBay users will use this facility in order to contact you. It is the safest way to communicate with other eBay members. All messages sent through this system are viewable by eBay customer support so if there is any kind of dispute you can ask customer support to examine the messages.

eBay will treat telephone conversations and emails sent outside of the messaging system as hearsay, so try to conduct all of your conversations through the messaging system.

To access the eBay messaging system:

1. Launch eBay
2. Sign in
3. Roll your mouse over the 'My eBay' link in the top right-hand corner of the page
4. Select 'Messages' from the bottom of the dropdown menu

You will soon realise that many of the queries you receive are very similar. Keep a Word document (or similar) with templates of your most used answers to speed up the process. Please see the 'Templates for communicating with your buyers' section later in this chapter for examples.

MOBILE APPLICATIONS

The eBay mobile app is a very worthwhile download if you are a smartphone user. It has various features that are of interest to an eBay seller, but it is especially useful for the message alerts. If you are an eBay app user you will be alerted instantly when you receive a message and you can respond via the app. This basically provides your buyer with a live chat facility, giving them instant access to you, and giving you the facility to respond to your customer's queries with lightning speed.

Tip

If you are a smartphone user, download the eBay and PayPal apps for access to your accounts on the move.

TEMPLATES FOR COMMUNICATING
WITH YOUR BUYERS

Day five payment reminder

POLITE REMINDER

Dear ***INSERT CUSTOMER'S NAME***,

It has been 5 days since you made a commitment to purchase this item and I haven't received payment.

If you would like to proceed with the transaction please send payment as soon as you can. If you would prefer to cancel the order please let me know and I can process the request.

If I do not receive payment or a response to this message within 48 hours I will open an unpaid item dispute.

If you have any questions or queries please do not hesitate to contact me. I am pleased to help in any way I can.

Where is my item?
'Same day 2nd Class service' response

Dear ***INSERT CUSTOMER'S NAME***

Your item was despatched on the day your purchase was completed on ***INSERT DATE OF DESPATCH*** by your chosen postal service of Royal Mail 2nd Class Post.

Items sent using this service usually take approximately 2–3 days from the date of despatch to arrive at their destination, but may take up to 14 working days. The Royal Mail will not entertain any claims for loss until 14 working days have passed from the date of despatch; at present only ***INSERT NUMBER OF DAYS*** working days have passed.

Please call your local sorting office as the item may have been returned there following a failed delivery attempt. If the item hasn't arrived by ***INSERT DATE*** and it is still not at the sorting office, please contact me again and I will submit a claim for loss with the Royal Mail and arrange despatch of a replacement or a full refund.

I am extremely sorry for any inconvenience, but once the parcel is handed to the Royal Mail it is beyond our control. For future purchases I would recommend using the 1st Class Postage option as items sent using this service are usually delivered on the next working day, claims for loss are able to be submitted after just 5 working days have passed from the date of despatch, and the extra financial outlay is minimal.

If I can assist further I am happy to help in any way I can, so please do not hesitate to contact me again.

Where is my item?
'Same day 1st Class service' response

Dear ***INSERT CUSTOMER'S NAME***

Your item was despatched on the day your purchase was completed on ***INSERT DATE OF DESPATCH*** by your chosen postal service of Royal Mail 1st Class Post.

Items sent using this service are usually delivered on the next working day, but may take up to 5 working days. The Royal Mail will not entertain any claims for loss until 5 working days have passed from the date of despatch; at present only ***INSERT NUMBER OF DAYS*** working days have passed.

Please call your local sorting office as the item may have been returned there following a failed delivery attempt. If the item hasn't arrived by ***INSERT DATE*** and it is still not at the sorting office, please contact me again and I will submit a claim for loss with the Royal Mail and arrange despatch of a replacement or a full refund.

I am extremely sorry for any inconvenience, but once the parcel is handed to the Royal Mail it is beyond our control. If I can assist further I am happy to help in any way I can, so please do not hesitate to contact me again.

Where is my item?
'Next day 2nd Class service' response

Dear ***INSERT CUSTOMER'S NAME***

Your item was despatched on the next working day after your payment was received on ***INSERT DATE OF DESPATCH*** by your chosen postal service of Royal Mail 2nd Class Post.

Items sent using this service usually take approximately 2–3 days from the date of despatch to arrive at their destination, but may take up to 14 working days. The Royal Mail will not entertain any claims for loss until 14 working days have passed from the date of despatch; at present only ***INSERT NUMBER OF DAYS*** working days have passed.

Please call your local sorting office as the item may have been returned there following a failed delivery attempt. If the item hasn't arrived by ***INSERT DATE*** and it is still not at the sorting office, please contact me again and I will submit a claim for loss with the Royal Mail and arrange despatch of a replacement or a full refund.

I am extremely sorry for any inconvenience, but once the parcel is handed to the Royal Mail it is beyond our control. For future purchases I would recommend using the 1st Class Postage option as items sent using this service are usually delivered on the next working day, claims for loss are able to be submitted after just 5 working days have passed from the date of despatch, and the extra financial outlay is minimal.

If I can assist further I am happy to help in any way I can, so please do not hesitate to contact me again.

Where is my item?
'Next day 1st Class service' response

Dear ***INSERT CUSTOMER'S NAME***

Your item was despatched on the next working day after your payment was received on ***INSERT DATE OF DESPATCH*** by your chosen postal service of Royal Mail 1st Class Post.

Items sent using this service are usually delivered on the next working day, but may take up to 5 working days. The Royal Mail will not entertain any claims for loss until 5 working days have passed from the date of despatch; at present only ***INSERT NUMBER OF DAYS*** working days have passed.

Please call your local sorting office as the item may have been returned there following a failed delivery attempt. If the item hasn't arrived by ***INSERT DATE*** and it is still not at the sorting office, please contact me again and I will submit a claim for loss with the Royal Mail and arrange despatch of a replacement or a full refund.

I am extremely sorry for any inconvenience, but once the parcel is handed to the Royal Mail it is beyond our control. If I can assist further I am happy to help in any way I can, so please do not hesitate to contact me again.

Where is my item?
'Same day courier' response

Dear ***INSERT CUSTOMER'S NAME***

Your item was despatched on the next working day after your payment was received on ***INSERT DATE OF DESPATCH*** by your chosen service of 3–5 day courier.

The tracking number for the parcel is: ***INSERT TRACKING No***

The parcel can be tracked at: ***INSERT WEB ADDRESS***

The tracking details to date are: ***INSERT UP-TO-DATE TRACKING DETAILS***

OPTIONALI have phoned the courier and they have requested that the parcel be reissued for delivery on ***INSERT DATE***. I hope this is convenient. If it is not, please let me know a date that is convenient for you.

OPTIONALAs you can see from the tracking details the parcel was delivered on ***INSERT DATE*** at ***INSERT TIME*** and signed for by ***INSERT NAME***. If you do not know this person or have not received your parcel please let me know so that I can raise the issue with the courier.

OPTIONALThe Courier still has ***INSERT NUMBER*** day(s) to complete the delivery.

OPTIONALItems sent using this service usually arrive within the allocated period, but sometimes things go wrong. I will contact the courier and report back to you as soon as I have any information.

If I can assist further I am happy to help in any way I can, so please do not hesitate to contact me again.

Damages

Dear ***INSERT CUSTOMER'S NAME***

I am extremely sorry that your item has arrived with you in less than perfect condition. All of our items are inspected prior to despatch and are packed in such a way to prevent damages. Unfortunately, our postal system is brutal and a very small percentage of items do not survive.

In order to speed up the refund/replacement process we request that you provide us with photos of:

1. The packaging exterior
2. The packaging interior
3. The Item in full
4. The damage sustained to the item

Please email the photos to ***INSERT EMAIL ADDRESS*** and we will submit a claim to the carrier. We will also issue your refund or dispatch your replacement, whichever you prefer.

Please be aware that we may require the item (with the original packaging) to be returned to us or sent to another alternative address if the carrier wishes to inspect the item.

Returns

Dear ***INSERT CUSTOMER'S NAME***

I am extremely sorry that you are displeased with your purchase. Please read our returns policy and terms and conditions of sale that are available to view on the listing for the item you purchased.

In order to return your item, please follow the steps below:

1. Go to My eBay. You may be asked to sign in
2. Click 'Won'
3. Next to your listing, select 'Return this item' from the dropdown menu
4. Select 'I want to return an item' and click 'Continue'
5. The 'Return an item' form appears
6. Review the next page and click 'Request return'
7. Wait for me to accept your request (usually within 24 hours)
8. Prepare your item for postage and click 'Continue'
9. Post the item

Your refund will be issued upon receipt of the returned item.

If I can assist further I am happy to help in any way I can, so please do not hesitate to contact me again.

 Tip

Never throw away post office receipts – they are your proof of postage and you may need them when you have to make a claim from the Royal Mail.

GETTING FEEDBACK

Your feedback rating is very important. It is a buyer's recommendation and the first point of call for a potential purchaser when assessing if they want to trade with you.

The feedback system has several different aspects to it:

RATING

Buyers can leave positive, neutral or negative feedback. They do not have to justify their decision – eBay relies on the buyer being a reasonable person.

COMMENT

Buyers can explain their reasons for providing the seller with their chosen feedback rating.

DETAILED SELLER RATINGS

In the DSRs, buyers can score a seller out of five stars based on the service they received in four different criteria:

Item as described

The buyer's opinion of how accurately you described your item compared to the item they received. Maintain a high score by ensuring that your items arrive in one piece, that you despatch the correct item and that you describe the item you are listing accurately.

Communication

This is the buyer's opinion of the speed, politeness and accuracy of your communications. Maintain a high score by responding quickly, accurately and politely to customer's queries. Buyers cannot rate you on this category if they have not communicated with you or received communication from you.

Despatch time

The buyer's opinion of how fast the item was despatched. This rating is not generally of great accuracy: the buyer will rate you on how fast their item arrives rather than how quickly you posted it, so you are reliant on your carrier to provide your customer with the service they expect. Unfortunately, it doesn't matter if you despatch the item within minutes of the order being placed: if your carrier then takes a week or more to deliver it, you will probably receive a low rating.

Postage & packaging charges

The buyer's opinion of the fairness of your P&P charges. Buyers do not like paying more than the stamp value: often they do not understand that packaging materials cost money.

Maintain a high score by ensuring that you are not over-charging your customers. Offering multiple purchase discounts or free postage will boost your buyer's opinion of the service they received with regards to this category. Buyers cannot rate you on this category if you sent their item with free postage and packaging, but beware of choosing this option as it will cost you more in eBay fees.

Sellers cannot leave negative or neutral feedback for buyers, but can choose not to leave feedback.

RECEIVING NEGATIVE OR NEUTRAL FEEDBACK

Bear in mind that there are people out there who cannot be pleased, whatever you do or how hard you try to please them. At some point you will receive unjustified negative feedback and you will receive low ratings you don't deserve. Unfortunately, there is little you can do about it. But do not be a slave to the customers: be fair and politely explain to them that you are being fair.

If you receive negative or neutral feedback you have a few courses of action to choose from:

Reply to the feedback received

Leave a polite reply to negative or neutral feedback explaining why you consider it to be unfair.

Request a feedback revision

If you feel that the buyer may choose to change the feedback rating you can write to them requesting a feedback revision and explaining why you would like them to revise their feedback.

👍 **Tip**

Reply to ALL negative and neutral feedback, and, if you can, negotiate with the buyer to see if they will remove it.

Apply to have the feedback comment removed

If you are of the opinion that the feedback is false or defamatory, or the comment contains language that is profane, abusive or derogatory, you can request that the feedback comment be removed. Unfortunately, although the comment will be removed, the rating and associated DSRs will remain.

Report it to eBay

If the feedback breaches certain criteria eBay will remove feedback entirely. The most popular reason is feedback extortion. eBay will remove the comment if you can prove that a buyer has threatened to leave negative feedback unless you provide them with:

- A full or partial refund
- A return that falls outside applicable legal requirements and conditions stated clearly in your listing
- Goods or services outside of the transaction

Another reason is feedback manipulation. eBay will remove feedback if a buyer repeatedly purchases items from you with the express intention of damaging your feedback or DSR scores.

A negative feedback that has a positive comment may be removed if you inform eBay customer services, and it is against the feedback policy for a member to leave three or more low DSRs with a positive feedback. This is extremely hard to prove, but if you contact eBay customer services they can check to see if a particular feedback breaches this policy.

REPLYING TO FEEDBACK RECEIVED

From your SMP Summary:

1. Click the 'Community' link in the top right-hand corner of the webpage
2. Click the link to the 'Feedback forum' in the navigation bar on the left-hand side
3. Click the link to 'Reply to Feedback Received'
4. Locate the feedback to which you wish to respond
5. Click the 'Reply' link on the right-hand side
6. Type your reply into the empty field
7. Click the 'Leave Reply' button

👍**Tip**

Be prepared to receive some negative feedback – you can't please all of the people all of the time.

REQUESTING A FEEDBACK REVISION

From your SMP Summary:

1. Click the 'Community' link in the top right-hand corner of the webpage
2. Click the link to the 'Feedback forum' in the navigation bar on the left-hand side

3. Click the link to 'Request Feedback Revision'
4. Locate the feedback that you would like your customer to revise
5. Click the 'Request revision' link on the right-hand side
6. Type your reasons for requesting the revision into the empty field
7. Click the 'Send Request' button

REPORTING FALSE AND DEFAMATORY FEEDBACK

From your SMP Summary:

1. Click the 'Customer Support' link in the top right-hand corner of the webpage
2. Type into the search engine 'defamation'
3. Click the 'Search' button
4. In the 'Related help' box click the link to 'Defamation claims'
5. Click the link to 'Download the Notice'
6. Print and complete it
7. Scan or photograph the completed form and save it into your computer (.gif, .jpg or .png format)
8. Click the link to 'Upload your document(s)'
9. Complete the process

REPORTING FEEDBACK EXTORTION

From your SMP Summary:

1. Click the 'Customer Support' link in the top right-hand corner of the webpage
2. Type into the search engine 'feedback extortion'
3. Click the 'Search' button
4. In the 'Related help' box click the link to 'Feedback extortion policy'

5.   Locate and click the link to 'report the suspected Feedback extortion'
6.   Complete the form
7.   Click the 'Send' button

REPORTING FEEDBACK MANIPULATION

From your SMP Summary:

1.   Click the 'Customer Support' link in the top right-hand corner of the webpage
2.   Type into the search engine 'feedback manipulation'
3.   Click the 'Search' button
4.   In the 'Related help' box click the link to 'Feedback manipulation policy'
5.   Locate and click the link to 'Report members who are trying to damage your (or another member's) Feedback score or detailed seller ratings'
6.   Complete the form
7.   Click the 'Send' button

FEEDBACK STAR ICON

The star icon located next to a feedback rating denotes the number of feedbacks that member has received. The colours of the stars change as the feedback rating increases:

Yellow star – 10 to 49 ratings
Blue star – 50 to 99 ratings
Turquoise star – 100 to 499 ratings
Purple star – 500 to 999 ratings
Red star – 1,000 to 4,999 ratings
Green star – 5,000 to 9,999 ratings

Yellow shooting star – 10,000 to 24,999 ratings
Turquoise shooting star – 25,000 to 49,999 ratings
Purple shooting star – 50,000 to 99,999 ratings
Red shooting star – 100,000 to 499,000 ratings
Green shooting star – 500,000 to 999,999 ratings
Silver shooting star – 1,000,000 ratings or more

POWERSELLER STATUS

There are five levels of Powerseller achievable: Bronze, Silver, Gold, Platinum and Titanium. The level you attain depends on your number of sales or value of sales within a set period of time. The requirements for the different types of Powerseller status are listed below:

Bronze – £2,000 worth of sales in twelve months and a minimum of 100 transactions

Silver – £4,500 in sales or 900 transactions in the previous three-month period, or £18,000 in sales or 3,600 transactions in the previous twelve months

Gold – £18,000 in sales or 3,000 transactions in the previous three-month period, or £72,000 in sales or 12,000 transactions in the previous twelve months

Platinum – £45,000 in sales or 7,500 transactions in the previous three-month period, or £180,000 in sales or 30,000 transactions in the previous twelve months

Titanium – £285,000 in sales or 15,000 transactions in the previous three-month period, or £1,140,000 in sales or 60,000 transactions in the previous twelve months

As a Powerseller, you also have the opportunity to qualify for eBay Top Rated Seller status, which recognises sellers who have a proven track record of excellent customer service and sales.

TOP RATED SELLER STATUS

To achieve eBay Top Rated Seller status you need to meet the following requirements:

1. Have an eBay account that's been active for at least ninety days
2. Have a positive feedback rating of at least 98 per cent
3. Be a member of the Powerseller programme
4. Adhere to eBay's Selling Practices Policy
5. Meet certain requirements for detailed seller ratings (DSRs) and eBay Buyer Protection/PayPal Buyer Protection cases

More information about these programmes can be found in the eBay help pages.

USING THE RESOLUTION CENTRE

The Resolution Centre is intended to be a last resort. It is an eBay-mediated forum in which the buyer and seller work out their differences to resolve the transaction in a mutually satis-factory manner. In theory, the aggrieved should attempt to communicate with the other party prior to opening a case. In practice, you will find that this is not always the way it works. Buyers will often skip straight to the resolution process. This is annoying, but better than the buyers leaving negative feedback without even attempting to resolve a problem.

eBay allows a set period for you and your buyer to resolve the issue before either party can refer the issue to customer support, who will then make a final decision.

SELLERS CAN OPEN A CASE IF:

They have not received payment

Do this if you find it necessary to open an unpaid item case for a transaction in which the buyer has not paid you.

They want to cancel a transaction

If you find it necessary to cancel a transaction for any reason, you can open a case with your buyer. This doesn't always have to be a dispute situation: it can be by prior mutual agreement with your buyer.

BUYERS CAN OPEN A CASE IF:

They haven't received their item

The buyer must wait a set period of time before the system will allow them to open this type of case. A buyer would usually have attempted to contact you via the messaging system prior to opening a case. They have either not received a response or not received the response they wanted to hear.

The item they received does not match the description

The buyer is of the opinion that the item differs significantly from the description. They may have received a damaged item or a wrong item, or they think that their purchase is not of the quality or value they expected.

They want to return the item

The buyer can return the item for any number of reasons. They may not necessarily have an issue with the item or service but no longer want to purchase it. In many cases, under the provisions of the Distance Selling Regulations Act, your buyer has seven days in which to notify you of their intent to return a purchase, for any reason, and you have to accept it.

 Tip

Assist your buyer as much as you can – you may even turn a negative experience into positive feedback.

OPENING A CASE

Unpaid items

We have already dealt with the issues behind opening an unpaid item case in the 'Invoicing Your Customers' section of Chapter 5. The process is described below:

1. Roll your mouse over the 'Customer Support' link in the top right-hand corner of the webpage
2. Click on the 'Resolution centre' link in the dropdown menu
3. Select 'I haven't received my payment yet'
4. Click the 'Continue' button
5. Enter the item number into the field (or click the 'Look for item number here' link, select the item number from the menu provided and click the 'Continue' button)
6. Click the 'Continue' button
7. Select the transaction for which you wish to open a case
8. Click the 'Continue' button

Cancellations

If you find it necessary to cancel a transaction for any reason, it is best to have already obtained agreement with your buyer. Occasionally a buyer will contact you requesting that you cancel the transaction: it is your responsibility to do so. Buyers cannot open a cancellation case. Cancellation cases do not count against you or the buyer when it comes to performance figures, so it is better to cancel than force a different type of dispute or receive negative feedback.

You will not lose out by cancelling a transaction as eBay will refund its fees to you.

To open a cancellation case:

1. Roll your mouse over the 'Customer Support' link in the top right–hand corner of the webpage
2. Click on the 'Resolution centre' link in the dropdown menu
3. Select 'I want to cancel a transaction'
4. Click the 'Continue' button
5. Enter the item number into the field (or click the 'Look for item number here' link, select the item number from the menu provided and click the 'Continue' button)
6. Click the 'Continue' button
7. Select the transaction you wish to cancel
8. Click the 'Continue' button
9. Select the reason for the cancellation from the dropdown menu
10. Type a message or further explanation into the field below if required
11. Click the 'Send request' button

IF A BUYER OPENS A CASE AGAINST YOU

You will receive a notification via the eBay messaging system in the event that a buyer opens a case against you.

The message will provide some details about the case. Click the button to 'Respond Now' and try to resolve the problem for your buyer.

Respond promptly and politely to the issue and to any further communications you may have from the buyer. Remember that any communications conducted via the eBay messaging system are able to be viewed by members of the customer support team, so if the buyer contradicts himself or changes his story, refer to the message in your response to the case.

If you are unable to resolve the problem within a set time period either you or the buyer can refer the case to customer support, who will adjudicate. It is in your interest to resolve the problem: you do not want eBay to judge in the buyer's favour.

Feel free to phone or live chat with an eBay advisor regarding your case. They will assist with any queries you may have and can advise you on what the correct course of action should be regarding your case.

APPENDIX: USEFUL LINKS

Below I have made reference to some of the internet web addresses that I have used with my eBay business. There are, of course, many other suppliers and providers available through various search engines. This is purely a taster to get you started.

Suppliers
www.gemwholesale.co.uk
www.efghousewares.co.uk
www.stockshifters.co.uk
www.thewholesaler.co.uk
www.autumnfair.com
www.springfair.com
www.sportsworld.co.uk
www.ikea.com
www.lidl.co.uk
www.aldi.co.uk

Communications
www.gmail.com
www.talktalk.com.uk

www.outlook.com
www.t-mobile.co.uk/business

Photography
www.fujifilm.eu/uk
www.photobucket.com

Postage & Packaging Services
www.royalmail.com/discounts-payment/discounts-packets-uk/
packetpost/faqs
www.royalmail.com/customer-service
www.parcel2go.com
http://stores.ebay.co.uk/Globe-Packaging

Equipment
www.hp.com

 Tip
Work hard and have fun! There's no point in doing it if you
don't enjoy it.

INDEX